Personality Disorders
and
Mental Illnesses

*The Truth About Psychopaths, Sociopaths, and
Narcissists!*

Clarence T. Rivers

Disclaimer: All attempts have been made by the author to provide factual and accurate content. No responsibility will be taken by the author or publisher for any damages caused by misuse of the content described in this book. The content of this book has been derived from various sources. Please consult an expert before attempting anything described in this book

TABLE OF CONTENTS

CONCLUSION

INTRODUCTION

Thank you for purchasing the book, *Personality Disorders and Mental Illnesses: The Truth About Psychopaths, Sociopaths, and Narcissists!*

There are several types of sickness that plague humankind, and some of them are not even physical. Like physical illnesses, mental illnesses cause health risks for people who obtain them. Some mental illnesses are enduring and ingrained, while others are temporary and easily treated. Regardless of the severity, sickness of the mind can cause a person to be unable to form social relationships or perform daily tasks. Afflicted individuals develop behavior that is unacceptable for social norms. There are those who survive mental illness, and there are those who succumb to it. There are known cases of people learning to live with it, but there are also incidents where attempts to overcome it fail, and lives are claimed as a result.

How common is it?

According to the World Health Organization (WHO), there are roughly 450 million people, on average, who are suffering from mental illness. A great percentage of these individuals are adolescents. Some of these people have suicidal tendencies, and successful suicides occur mostly in poverty stricken countries and places with generally cold climates.

Research shows that suicide cases alone have risen by 60% in the last 45 years, with victims' ages ranging from 15 to 40 years old.

It is for this and many other significant reasons that medication and professional counselling are sought and provided in most developed countries. Medication can help in dealing with several types of mental illnesses, although prior counselling is required, while natural alternatives are preferred by others.

How is mental illness obtained? Where does it come from?

Mental illnesses are not instantly developed; they occur due to a combination of many factors, including personal experiences combined over the course of years or months. Some are easily noticeable with identifiable causes, but others are slow to develop and might only show seemingly harmless symptoms like mild depression.

Not only is the whole of the individual an important factor, but his or her surroundings can also determine the character or severity of the mental illness. Climate, culture, and social experiences, especially childhood experiences, are some of the external forces that psychiatrists consider when diagnosing people with mental illness. Some illnesses are primary effects of traumatic experiences, while others are inherited in genes. Some are transient or temporary, while others are recurring, even chronic. One cannot prevent the occurrence of mental illness in a person since there is more than one factor that helps to develop it.

There are different forms of treatment that help cure mental illness. There are also alternative methods for those who prefer natural ways to cure the condition. Depending on the severity and type of mental illness, the afflicted person might undergo medication, psychotherapy, group therapy, or hospitalization. There are existing *natural* alternatives that claim to help with such illnesses, like meditative strategies, body massages, and even water therapy.

Nowadays, people often use the term "psychopath" to refer to criminals and people with violent tendencies. However, this abusive use of the word has led people to believe that any two-bit criminal immediately falls under the psychopath category.

There are nuances to the definition of psychopathy that are often ignored due to the sensationalized use of the term. Here's a simple reminder: not all psychopaths are criminals, and not all criminals are psychopaths. In fact, you may have an acquaintance that can be considered a psychopath—or you might be a psychopath yourself.

Regardless of these misconceptions (or perhaps because of them), psychopathy is a fascinating subject for most people. This book aims to set the record straight once and for all about psychopathy, and how exactly the mind of a psychopath works.

This book is divided into several chapters, which discuss each specific aspect of psychopathy. You can learn all about Anti-Social Personality Disorder (ASPD) as well as signs and symptoms of psychopathic behavior in one chapter. Another chapter differentiates psychopaths from sociopaths according to certain defining characteristics of these two psychological disorders. Several chapters of this book also discuss behavioral patterns associated with psychopathy, including narcissism and violence, among others.

Delve into the minds of the world's most famous psychopaths and discover the twisted logic that makes them commit horrific crimes without showing any signs of remorse. Why do they enjoy inflicting pain and suffering on other people, without qualms or any twinges of conscience?

You can find everything you need to know about psychopaths and psychopathy in this book. Plus, find out if you have psychopathic tendencies yourself by taking the Psychopath Test!

Now, lets switch gears and explore Sociopathy.

Is society to be blamed for the negative perception of sociopaths? It is undeniable that serial killers and notorious criminals throughout history have proven sociopaths can be extremely dangerous individuals. Their presence itself is threatening, and they must be handled with great precaution. While they can be fearsome and their existence is troubling, they do stir intrigue. We cannot help but wonder about their natures, simply because they are different. They are far from normal.

In reading this book, you have to keep this in mind: sociopathy is defined as a syndrome that makes a person incapable of emotionally conditioning his or her social experiences. Sociopaths essentially lack the ability to emotionally organize. This is why they do not feel empathy or other feelings that are normal to other people.

In other words, sociopaths are different. If someone in your life seems different, find out through this book whether or not it is cause for alarm.

By understanding how the mind of a sociopath works, you become capable of protecting yourself against manipulation, deception, and possible physical harm. Throughout this book, you can turn from a potentially easy victim to an individual who can defy attempts of control even from a person who seems genuine and charismatic.

Being different is not always bad. It goes without saying that not all sociopaths turn out to be serial killers or criminals. Find out who to protect yourself from.

Finally, I'd like to discuss the growing epidemic of Narcissism. As you cross the street, you are very likely to come across a narcissist, and this means one thing: they are common. Of course, there are two sides of the coin when it comes to this type of personality.

There is the captivating individual who can be an inspiration to many, once you look past the vanity. And then, there is the artful and short-tempered narcissist who suffers from so much self-love that he cannot accept the fact that not everyone agrees with him. Nevertheless, it is best to get to know more about this interesting phenomenon–or disorder, whichever you view it to be–and learn how to handle anyone in your life who is a narcissist.

This segment will provide you with all the inform-ation that you will need in order to understand narcissism and the narcissistic personality disorder. Here, you be able to find out how to identify someone who is a narcissist (or if you are one yourself), read up on ideas about whether this is a good or a bad thing (or a little bit of both), and how to control yourself if you are narcissistic.

Narcissism has become an increasingly controversial and popular topic due to the rise of media that promote this type of behavior. This book seeks to open up the mind of a narcissist and let you peek into it and see what's going on.

After all, now that more and more individuals are regularly posting "selfies" (short for self portraits, usually taken with a camera) and boasting about their accomplishments on the internet, could it be that narcissism has become a norm? It is amazing what you can learn from the mind of a narcissist. You will make many new discoveries about yourself and society once you have read this book.

So without further ado, let's dive right in!

Thanks again,

CHAPTER 1

Personality Disorders and Mental Illnesses

There are many types of mental illnesses; there are those that affect mood, personality, and psyche. Some of these mental illnesses, like eating disorders, can be overcome or prevented with the support of loved ones, while others require professional help. There are also critical conditions that require medication, psychiatric counselling and/or therapy.

Common Types of Mental Illness

One of the most popular, if not easily distinguishable mental illnesses, is phobia. A phobia is a type of anxiety disorder where the person afflicted has an irrational fear of an object, animal, or situation. When the person is confronted with the object of his or her fear, he or she will take great measures to keep away from it. When confrontation is inevitable, the person experiences panic attacks or feel greatly distressed.

General phobia is an irrational or unexplainable fear of the many dangers of life. General phobia is usually characterized by the fear of uncontrollable events, like death, and general threats such as natural disasters, murder, accidents, and epidemics. People with general phobia also have anxiety and tend to become restless—especially at night—because of over-thinking and over-worrying.

There are specific types of phobias that are focused on a particular object or situation, such as the fear of spiders (arachnophobia) and the fear of confined spaces (claustrophobia). Some fears are not just irrational, but also very unusual, like Tremophobia (fear of trembling), Amaxophobia (fear of riding cars), and Anthrophobia (fear of flowers).

The most common phobias are as follows:

- Arachnophobia (fear of arachnids)
- Acrophobia (fear of heights or seeing heights)
- Cynophobia (fear of dogs)
- Astraphobia (fear of thunder and lightning)

- Pteromerhanophobia (fear of flying in planes, helicopters, etc.)

.

Rare Types of Mental Illnesses

Some mental illnesses are rare, but the severity of such conditions is extreme, making them infamous in the medical world. There are also psychotic disorders that don't just affect a person's behavior, but also the brain and its cognitive thinking. This type of mental illness interferes with "reality" in the eyes of the person, making him or her unable to live normally in any way. For example, schizophrenia is a condition in which a person has more than one personality and an inability to tell reality apart from fantasy.

Another known but rare condition is the infamous Manic Bipolar Disorder. People with schizophrenia develop delusional beliefs that start out as simple fantasies that later take over their lives almost completely. Sometimes, these delusions are involuntary. In addition, schizophrenics have a complicated set of behaviors and ways of thinking. Not only are schizophrenics *paranoid*, they may also be *depressive* and *anxious,* but in such extreme levels that they can neither think clearly, nor face choices or changes.

Schizophrenia

The main characteristics of schizophrenia are disorganized thinking, severe paranoia and/or anxiety, and a disconnection from reality. People with this condition experience hallucinations: hearing voices or seeing apparitions that are not really there. When told that these experiences are unreal, a schizophrenic might deny the truth to the extent of becoming aggressive. Schizophrenic individuals also experience phantom pains. The unreal experiences affect their way of thinking, disrupting it and leading them to disbelieve others, even loved ones.

Confusion is inevitable in this condition, and cognitive thinking is greatly affected. This kind of mental illness not only affects the afflicted person, but also the people around him or her. They are not mentally capable of doing certain jobs. It is unsafe for them to be left alone, and it is also unsafe for them to be in crowded places. People who are diagnosed with schizophrenia are considered self-destructive, and they may also pose a possible threat to others. The schizophrenic individual is not just emotionally unstable, but has no strength to control their illness, making them unpredictable and sometimes prone to inhumane actions.

There are four types of schizophrenics:

Disorganized Type - this type of schizophrenia is characterized by general disorganization. People with this type of disorder suddenly talk gibberish or recite songs, poems, or scripts, and they do so for no apparent reason. They might even invent a language of their own or simply speak out meaningless words. Some will suddenly laugh, sob, or giggle by themselves, obviously caught up and lost in their own thoughts.

Paranoid Type – paranoid type schizophrenics have extreme anxiety and fear. Their paranoia revolves around the suspicion that someone, a surreal being or secret organization, is out to capture or hurt them. A paranoid schizophrenic may also feel that others are harassing him or are scheming to overthrow, murder, or harm him in some way. People who are paranoid schizophrenic have a tendency to argue excessively with others, act aloof, and display fits of anger or rage. They have the unusual belief that there is either a known or unknown enemy nearby.

Undifferentiated Type – this type has some of the characteristics of the other types of schizophrenia. The individual may have paranoid symptoms as well as disorganization. What makes this type of schizophrenic separate is that the symptoms are not equally evident and are only transitional, if not temporary, and no symptoms are intense enough to categorize the person under a single type.

Residual Type – this simply means "leftovers" of a previous or past history of schizophrenia in a person. There are some symptoms of the condition left that may indicate a major outburst followed by complete remission, or simply no more occurrences for the rest of the individual's life.

Manic Bipolar Disorder

This disorder is infamous for its extremely noticeable characteristics. Like schizophrenics, manic-bipolar individuals have a false sense of reality and tend to live in their own thoughts of fantasy. People with this condition believe they are an entirely different person; for example, the Queen of Sheba, an ex-convict hiding from government forces, or an alien envoy from another galaxy. Their perception of reality is so altered that they have no sense of time, place, or what is happening to them. Manic bipolar individuals will suddenly act a certain way without warning, possibly hurting others. Some individuals with bipolar disorder simply stop moving or speaking for hours.

Infamous cases involve individuals talking non-sensical things, putting make-up on, and dressing in unusual ways. Some of the most serious cases involve the individual stopping in the middle of his or her activities, including walking. The person maintains this "pose" for hours without disturbance. Others may try to provoke the individual to move or speak, but to no avail. The danger in this is that the return of motion is unpredictable; it may take days before the manic bipolar resumes his activities, and sometimes when he does, he is aggressive.

Schizophrenia and manic bipolar disorder are chronic mental illnesses that require multiple medications alongside psychotherapy and moral support. Some cases take years to treat, and most individuals with these disorders experience recurring symptoms with remissions before finally achieving more stable mental health. Remissions are lingering episodes or periods of time when the afflicted individual experiences a mentally healthy state. The symptoms of their illness are absent for a time being, but the cycle ends at some point, and the onset of the symptoms returns. Not all mental illnesses have remissions; some are consistent, while other symptoms grow less in severity but are still present.

Understanding Personality Disorder

Mental illnesses vary; some are extreme and prolonged, while others are recurring but mild. Differences in consistency and severity set the types of mental illness apart from each other. Personality disorders are a kind of mental illness. They are focused on, but not specifically confined to, the behavior of the individual. While most mental illnesses have many symptoms in common, they are different by contrast and degree.

Differences Between Mental Illness and Personality Disorder

Personality disorders fall under a class of mental illness that is recognizable by patterns in human behavior. These patterns are out of the ordinary. In comparison to what most people would normally do in their culture, a person with a personality disorder feels, thinks, perceives, and relates differently. This *different* behavior is usually obvious, either because of its extremity in nature or lack of extremities. A person suffering from this kind of condition is capable of working and forming relationships, but with difficulty.

What is personality disorder?

Personality disorder is the condition where one's overall personality is affected by his or her thoughts and behavior. There is a pattern in the behavior that is self-destructive or dissocial in nature. Its character-istics are not acceptable to most people. The signs and symptoms begin forming during the younger years, but only become noticeable later. Signs are often evident in the workplace, where social interaction and a variety of other forces are at work, like change, pressure, and criticism. The signs and symptoms of personality disorders are much easier to see in this type of environment.

How are personality disorders obtained?

People get conditions like these during their adolescent years, when experiences are most memorable and influential. Most mental conditions are obtained during this stage. Personality disorders develop from adolescence, but come to light or worsen during adulthood.

The classification of personality disorders is argued over by most institutions and psychiatric organizations because of their nature. People with personality disorder may carry the condition throughout their lives; there is a characteristic that suggests that untreated or mistreated cases grow steadily worse. People with personality disorders are also most prone to acquiring other types of mental illnesses, in addition to suicidal tendencies and substance abuse.

The Four Clusters/Types of Personality Disorder (Clusters A & B)

Personality disorders are organized into four clusters. In each cluster, there are three to four conditions. These conditions also have subtypes with unique behavioral patterns; however, these will not be included.

Cluster A

The first cluster, Cluster A Personality Disorder, is made up of personality disorders that make an individual unable to relate to others. People with personality disorders in this cluster are usually defined as "odd," "strange," or "eccentric." They are described by others as people who seem to have a world of their own.

Paranoid

Paranoia is a condition where the person is constantly wary of his or her surroundings. Paranoid individuals generally mistrust others; some types of paranoid people will take extreme measures to ensure their safety through preparations like stockpiling food or weapons in the home. People with this condition tend to suspect bad things are about to happen; some of these fears are legitimate, while others are imaginary. One of the most extreme behaviors of paranoid people is extensively searching for evidence in their surroundings to validate their fears or suspicions. They are constantly on the look-out for signs of danger, scanning for possible escape routes in case these dangers occur. Paranoid individuals also tend to have explosive tempers; this is a defense mechanism that triggers when the individual feels apprehensive.

The causes of paranoia differ for each person. Most cases develop due to negative feelings, starting from bad parental models and leading to peer rejection and social insecurity. There are also genetic contributions to this condition. Some people with schizophrenia tend to develop paranoia and vice versa.

Schizoid

Often mistaken as schizophrenia, schizoid personality disorder is more passive in nature and not as prolonged. A person with schizoid personality disorder is distant, not only emotionally, but also socially. People with this condition are solitary and secretive. In addition to that, they are apathetic, even when it comes to social and romantic relationships. Ironically, these individuals are passive and inferior. They prefer solace because they are afraid of emotional intimacy. This disorder is rare, and some psychologists argue that its diagnosis depends on a place's cultural norms. In some countries, this type of behavior is acceptable—not necessarily normal, but not far above or below what is considered "sane."

Negligence during childhood and extremely perfectionist parenting are the main causes of schizoid personality disorders. Other causes point to genetic inheritance.

Schizotypal

Quite like the schizoid, a person with schizotypal personality disorder seeks social isolation. He or she may develop odd behaviors that others see as strange, like dressing up unusually or talking to themselves. The difference between schizoid and schizotypal is that the latter has more of an ability to converse socially, but in an odd manner, which makes it difficult for the person to form relationships. Schizotypal individuals also usually have interesting beliefs, such as those in the paranormal field.

Schizotypal traits are usually developed early in childhood. Negative experiences, such as early separation from the parents, trauma, and negligence, are major causes. Genetic inheritance is also a contributor.

Cluster B

Cluster B of personality disorders involves conditions that cause dramatic and erratic behaviors. People with Cluster B disorders have difficulty in regulating their emotions. They tend to have extreme mood swings, become overly dramatic, impulsive, and generally unpredictable. Their instability is not only visible in their emotions, but is also evident in the relationships they form.

Antisocial

Antisocial personality disorder is also known as dissocial personality disorder. Antisocial individuals are seen by most as being purposefully juvenile and disruptive. They have no regard for the rights or personal space of others. Most people with antisocial personality disorder have criminal records. They seek to go in the opposite direction of what is accepted as normal. They are also prone to substance abuse and have a tendency for violence.

There are many possible causes for a person to become antisocial. The surroundings, including social influences, play a heavy role in that. Psychiatrists also consider hormonal imbalance to be a major contributor.

Borderline

Borderline personality disorder is among the most well known personality disorders. The person with this disorder is characterized as emotionally unstable or emotionally intense. They can be impulsive or have outbursts during random situations. Unlike how normal people are, those with borderline personality disorder are more deeply in tune with their emotions. They feel more intensely, quicker, and longer than average, regardless of the situation. They are also noticeably sensitive to criticism, rejection, abandonment, and neglect.

People with borderline personality have unhealthy relationships. They put their partners in unpredictable situations, displaying extreme pleasure or extreme disappointment to their partner. This personality disorder is characterized by intense mood swings that are destructive when handled incorrectly.

Borderline individuals are usually depressed and may resort to self mutilation during extreme emotional episodes. Being easily swayed by negative emotions coupled with an inability to handle rejection, they can be suicidal. Conversely, some might handle rejection differently, becoming manipulative to regain control of the relationship or loved one. They are especially attached to their partners when feeling alone or suspecting a lack of interest, love, or care. Self harm is perceived by the individual as a means to end the "feeling." Most of the time, borderline individuals will "zone out" and retreat into their thoughts in an unconscious attempt to block out intense emotions.

It is widely debated as to what the main causes of borderline personality disorder are. The factors are usually complex for each patient; some have had experiences of childhood trauma or suffer from post-traumatic disorder. Others show significant environ-mental and social influences.

Histrionic

Histrionics basically have little to no sense of self-worth. Primarily, they dramatize for attention and seem to be playing roles most of the time. People with this disorder seek approval or praise from others, and the way they behave to acquire this attention is generally inappropriate. As attention seekers, histrionics can be overly charming, seductive, or very flirtatious. They crave stimulation and excitement, using manipulative behavior to achieve it. Their search for stimulation and excitement usually puts them in situations where they can be exploited. Since promiscuousness is also a characteristic of histrionics, the exploitation is repetitive.

Despite a lack of self-worth, histrionic individuals are ironically very mindful of their appearance and physical presentation. Oftentimes, there is ego-centrism and self indulgence involved. Apparently, the need for approval is to ensure the survival of their ego.

Relationships are very unstable and short-lived; there is an exaggeration of intimacy on the affected person's part. A mnemonic that is used to easily describe a histrionic is the phrase "Praise me," which refers to the attention-seeking and egocentric character of the ill person.

So far, there isn't enough evidence that points to how histrionic personality disorder develops. Some studies show similarities in histrionic cases involving extravagance and vanity. One of the theories of what contributes greatly to histrionic personality disorder is abnormal lustfulness. In the psychoanalysis of Freud, this lustfulness is caused by the conditional love or emotional shallowness of the parents or guardians.

Narcissistic

Narcissistic personality disorder is characterized by exaggerated self-importance. The name for the disorder is derived from Greek mythology's Narcissus, who became entranced by his own beauty (seeing his reflection in the water) and dying because of it (he never left nor stopped looking at his reflection). Narcissistic individuals feel that others are envious of them, but they are also envious of others they perceive as being better or having more than they do. Selfish, self-centered, and manipulative, narcissistic individuals are also susceptible to seek revenge when they feel they are being slighted. This makes relationships with narcissists impossible to maintain.

They may also display fits of rage or outbursts when ridiculed. They have the notion that others cannot be more right than they are. In romantic relationships, people suffering from narcissistic personality disorder are manipulative and may have a habit of keeping tabs on *who's right and who's wrong.* There is an irrational and unrealistic expectation of praise, admiration, and attention from others. They also talk a great deal about themselves, are arrogant, and lack true empathy for other people.

This personality disorder stems from excessive praises and admiration from parents and relatives during childhood. Children who are overvalued and overindulged are most likely to develop narcissistic personality disorder. Emotional abuse as a child and experiences of manipulative behavior in parents are also contributing factors.

The Four Clusters/Types of Personality Disorder (Clusters C & D)

Cluster C

The third cluster of personality disorders, Cluster C, consists of conditions that are characterized by fearful and anxious natures. The main associated behavioral problems are withdrawal from society and avoidance due to heightened fears and anxiety. The presence of anxiety and fear is persistent, and the person suffering from this condition struggles on a regular basis. People with personality disorders in this cluster are particularly shy or withdrawn in nature and may have difficulty maintaining close relationships due to insecurity or anxiety.

Avoidant

Avoidant personality disorder is also known as anxious personality disorder. People with this condition avoid social interactions in general and don't deal well with criticism. Unlike paranoia, avoidant personality disorder is characterized by social anxiety instead of general anxiety. A person with this condition has low self esteem and feels that he or she is socially awkward. The reason for withdrawing from socializing is the fear of being humiliated or disliked by people. There is a general feeling of being unwanted, despite the lack of trying to socialize. Some are not only extremely shy, but have severe trust issues. Others develop self-loathing and self-criticism due to constant contemplation.

This condition is developed in both childhood and early adolescent years. Rejection by peers and public humiliation are common causes of this condition.

Dependent

Much like the name suggests, dependent personality disorder can be characterized by submissiveness and the tendency to rely on others to handle life in general. People with this disorder perceive others to be stronger, smarter, and more adept at handling different situations than them. Regardless of the ill person's own capabilities or skills, he or she prefers to let others take the lead, especially in romantic relationships.

The trouble with this condition is that the person afflicted has no confidence whatsoever that he or she can go on independently. In this person's perception, it is impossible, if not extremely unbearable, to have no one to "care" for him to whom he must submit, even to unreasonable demands. People with this condition often get along with others who are unpredictable or equally isolated.

As partners, they are meek, very submissive, and have no individuality. They can be considered as martyrs of the relationship, serving their partners hand and foot, even overlooking the abusive qualities of their partner. There is so much fear of abandonment that those afflicted will do almost anything to preserve their dependant relationship. This condition is chronic and can last throughout the person's life if not treated or confronted. The only viable cause for this condition is experiencing clinging parental behavior.

Obsessive-Compulsive Personality

This personality disorder is not the same as obsessive compulsive disorder. Obsessive-compulsive *personality* disorder is a condition in which the person afflicted strives for perfection and orderliness, while those suffering from obsessive compulsive disorder see their own ritualistic behavior as undesirable or wrong.

People with OCPD (Obsessive-Compulsive Personality Disorder) have a tendency to be overly concerned with perfection, orderliness, and control, not only with oneself, but also with one's environment. They usually have involuntary thoughts that intrude even during hours of rest, which makes it impossible for them to be calm or relax. There is always a need and *want* for order and predictability, which is why people with OCPD have difficulty in forming relationships.

While it's true that they can be very responsible and capable partners, their preference for perfection can drive their partners away. OCPD individuals greatly fear the unknown, beyond how an average person does. There is always a fear of new experiences, situations, and changes. Their uncontrollable anxieties are internal and involuntary. Oftentimes, this causes compulsive behaviors, such as excessive body cleaning.

In their minds, excessive cleanliness will prevent them from health deterioration, and keeping everything organized will ensure the safety and balance of their mental and emotional well-being. The reason OCPD falls under Cluster C is due to their constant feelings of helplessness and powerlessness regarding a variety of things. The effect of this helplessness is an attempt to gain control over oneself and one's environment. While the attempt is bold and well-meaning, the result is often unstable and unhealthy. Relationships are shaky because of mistrust. People with OCPD are also usually serious, miserly, and doubting, as well as humorless.

Childhood psychological trauma that is triggered by another negative event in one's life causes OCPD in most people. Such psychological trauma may include include sexual, physical, and emotional abuse during childhood. An influential environment can worsen the condition. Psychiatrists believe that OCPD can be copied from others who are very close to the individual. Repetitive and ritualistic behaviors can be learned from others and incorporated.

Cluster D

Cluster D includes personality disorders that have random characteristics belonging to two or more of the disorders from the other three clusters. These types of personality disorders are difficult to predict, as their symptoms are not as frequent or obvious when they show. These disorders are usually the result of only one personality disorder at its worst state, which, in its extremity, has developed another personality disorder.

For example, borderline personalities have a tendency for manipulation when feeling unloved or insecure. At the height of uncontrolled emotions, they have a tendency for paranoia and even histrionic personality disorder. These disorders are closely related because of their symptoms: *insecurity, distrust, disbelief,* and *erratic* or *uncontrollable emotions.*

Signs, Symptoms, and Sub-factors of Mental Illness

The most common signs and symptoms of an impending or present mental illness are depression, anxiety, paranoia, insecurity, and withdrawal from society. These are also the sub-factors that contribute to the development of mental illness in a person. These symptoms or sub-factors are normally found in meek people or people with low self esteem, but this does not imply that they suffer from a mental illness. To be considered mentally ill, a person's symptoms must be of above normal levels, meaning extreme.

Depression

Depression is a mood in which a person feels down due to a certain thought or situation. Prolonged depression or general depression is one of the common signs and symptoms of mental illness. Most mentally ill individuals are regularly depressed or experience loneliness and low self esteem. This contributes to the development of negative thoughts that can become involuntary overtime.

Anxiety

People can be anxious about any one thing with good reason. People who are mentally ill are anxious and have fears without valid reason, and if there are reasons, they are usually irrational or exaggerated. They react to the feared object or situation with such vigor that it's possible they might hurt others or get hurt themselves.

Their surroundings, and people in their surroundings, are often disregarded, and the only thing that matters is the need to escape from their source of fear. In the case of anxiety, mentally ill people are so anxious that they may experience insomnia due to constant worrying.

Paranoia

Paranoia is a disorder in itself, and it can be a sign or symptom of a more serious type of mental illness. Paranoia has no rational explanation for its fears, as with severe anxiety. Afflicted individuals will go to any means to avoid the feared object, or they will experience panic attacks when faced with it.

Withdrawal from Society

In most cultures, loners and anti-social individuals are not considered abnormal, only unusual. Withdrawal from society as a symptom of mental illness is usually an intense version of average lonesomeness. Avoidant people who have difficulty forming or keeping relationships and are downright antisocial are most prone to developing personality disorders. Most personality disorders share social incapability symptoms. The lack of social interaction gives more space for solace, which, while beneficial for self reflection, is not good in combination with depression and anxiety.

Without moral support or social connections, people experiencing depression and severe anxiety will have no one to help ease their inner suffering. Solace provides space for negative thinking, which enhances the overall mood of the individual, deepening depression and heightening anxiety.

Prevention, Treatment and Overcoming

The best way to overcome mental illness, whether minor or severe, is to have moral support throughout the duration of therapy or medication. Since most conditions stem from negative and traumatic childhood experiences, there is a need for positive replacement. A person whose memory and thinking is scarred by negligence, abuse, or maltreatment will most likely develop undesirable characteristics that can alter his or her personality. Since life experiences and people are unpredictable, at some point, an occurrence could trigger the development of a mental disorder.

CHAPTER 2

Psychopathy Defined

Psychopathy has always been a fascinating subject not only for psychologists and psychiatrists, but also for many people from different professions, and even to the regular pedestrian. Law enforcement officers, forensics experts, and criminologists are particularly invested in this topic because more often than not, psychopathy is associated with violent and horrendous crimes. It has also been the subject of numerous films and novels, both critically acclaimed and of the two-bit gore variety.

However, the creative license that many writers and directors have taken on this subject has blurred the lines between reality and myth when it comes to psychopaths and psychopathy in general. Nowadays, people tend to use the term psychopath to refer to almost all criminals who have committed crimes like rape and murder. This misconception cannot be more wrong.

Cultural Grounding: Views and Myths about Psychopathy

You've heard everything about psychopaths. They are on the news and in the movies, and you're scared to death of them because they're mad as hatters and crazy as hell. They don't think the same way as regular people, and they thrive on inflicting pain and torture on others: a   serial killer on the loose who enjoys toying with his victims before   killing them; a rapist who mutilates his victims before having sex with them; a deranged teenager who takes a shotgun and shoots everyone in sight; a cannibal who relishes writing the details of his exploits to the families of his victims.

Because of the sensationalism of the media, psychopathy has become a widely-feared and often misunderstood psychological disorder. The term has been used too loosely to refer to people who've committed heinous crimes, when in fact, psychologists have constructed a set of criteria and diagnostic tools specifically used to diagnose psychopathy.

When you think about it, there are a lot of misconceptions and myths about psychopathy in society, including the following:

Psychopathy means violence. Many people believe that all psychopaths are aggressive individuals with violent tendencies, and that all of them are criminals capable of committing horrendous crimes. While it is true that a fraction of imprisoned criminals have shown symptoms of psychopathy, research suggests that most psychopaths walk freely among "normal" people.

Psychopathy means psychosis. Most people seem to think that all   psychopaths are insane. This view is only reinforced by fictional psychopaths in popular culture, such as Batman's nemesis, The Joker, and the cannibal Hannibal.

Psychopathy has no cure. People who suffer from this condition are believed to be hopeless cases, and that there is no way to change their views and ways of thinking.

Not only are these ideas mostly wrong, they also contribute to the widespread public hysteria regarding psychopathic criminals and the supposed dangers that they pose to mankind. Throughout this book, we will slowly debunk each of these myths to create a more rational view of psychopathy and to form a clearer understanding of this condition.

The Truth about Psychopathy: Facts and Figures

The term psychopathy was coined in 1941 by a psychiatrist named Hervey M. Cleckley to describe specific traits and behavioral patterns. In a nutshell, psychopaths are said to be charming and seemingly normal at first—but they have an underlying callousness and egoism that make them capable of doing hurtful things simply for the sake of fun and enjoyment. All they care about is their personal well-being, and they don't mind lying or doing whatever it takes to get what they want.

Psychopaths are highly rational, but they are known to be undependable and irresponsible because they don't exhibit regular human emotions like empathy, guilt, or even love. They are very impulsive, and when things go wrong in their plans, they'll find someone else to take the blame for them. They don't listen to the words of other people and will continue head-on with their own plans.

Psychopaths are easily lured into criminal activity when they think they will be able to get away with it. Calculating, devious, and controlling, psychopaths are very dangerous when crossed. Psychopaths make up roughly 1% of the global population, and studies suggest that the majority of them are male.

It is true that many criminals can be considered psychopaths—one study suggests that an estimated 25%, or 1 out of 4 criminals in jail meet the diagnostic criteria for psychopathy. But these criminals are surely not the only psychopaths that walk the earth, are they?

In fact, most psychopaths are not criminals—and one might even be close to you. If not for their tendency to develop erratic and impulsive behaviors, a lot of psychopaths would be successful in their careers.

That being said, psychopaths tend to find high-flying and glamorous jobs more appealing than regular ones since having an impressive job strokes their egos. Corporate CEO-ship, lawmaking and enforcement, politics, clergy, and media practice are all potentially attractive job prospects for a psychopath.

Characteristics and Traits of a Psychopath

Psychiatrists and psychologists alike have come up with several diagnostic instruments to gauge psychopathy. Cleckley himself has devised a list of traits often displayed by psychopaths. A Canadian psychologist, Robert Hare, also created the Psychopathy Checklist-Revised (PCL-R), a popular 20-question checklist used to diagnose the incidence of psychopathy.

There is a general consensus among these diagnostic instruments about the common traits of a psychopath. The list includes the following traits, tendencies, and behavioral patterns. Some dominant behavioral patterns will be discussed in further detail in another chapter of this book.

Charm and intelligence: Psychopaths are smooth talkers, and they easily turn on a superficial kind of charm that leaves a false good impression on the people they meet. They are very verbose, and you'd never find one who gets tongue-tied or shy around other people.

Egocentrism/Narcissism: In a psychopath's way of thinking, the world revolves around them. Everything has to be about them: their needs, their wants, their desires. Anything else beyond that doesn't exist for them.

Pathological lying: At the very least, a psychopath may simply be cunning, shrewd, or clever. At the most, psychopaths have a tendency to carry out full-blown deceptions and manipulating others for their own interests. They can be underhanded, and because of their shallowness, they are without scruples in their deception tactics.

Easily bored, needing constant stimulation: Psychopaths are thrill-seekers. They thrive on excitement and danger. They love taking risks and tend to get bored with routine. This is why most psychopaths find it difficult to hold on to jobs and end up drifting on the fringes of society.

Manipulation and conning: Once they're sure that they can get away with it, psychopaths tend to use their deception techniques to control other people for personal gain. Cheating and fraudulent activities may be typical fare for a manipulative psychopath.

Guiltless and remorseless: Psychopaths don't feel any twinges of conscience for what they have done, because they have no value judgment abilities, and a warped sense of right and wrong. The only emotion they may display towards other people (or their victims) is disdain.

Callousness/No empathy: Psychopaths tend to be generally cold-hearted and unable to connect emotionally to other people. They don't feel concern or empathy regarding the damages they may have inflicted on other people, and they never feel a sense of loss. Psychopaths are often inconsiderate of other people's needs, and can be ruthless and tactless.

Shallow emotions and an inability to feel (especially love): A psychopath technically isn't a robot devoid of emotions, but he's close to one. He doesn't feel things the way "normal" people do. Although he might appear gregarious and even affectionate, his range of feelings and emotions is limited to the point of being nonexistent.

Poor or no temper control: Psychopaths often have anger management issues and violent tendencies precisely because they cannot control their behavior and expressions. They easily show signs of annoyance, anger, irritation, and impatience with other people, sometimes even with explosive and dangerous bouts of threatening and verbal and physical abuse.

Predatory/Parasitic: Psychopaths feed on other people. Because they often have unstable lives and careers, they intentionally find someone to manipulate to do their bidding. Instead of working to support themselves, they choose to use someone else to ensure their financial security. They can't hold regular jobs because they are looking for something grander (and more exciting) for themselves.

Sexual promiscuity: Psychopaths are almost mechanical when it comes to sex and relationships. They are impersonal and often cold to their partners; to psychopaths, each partner is just another conquest and ego booster. They have multiple partners in their lifetimes, and they don't really feel love or affection for any of them.

Impulsiveness: Psychopaths are very easy to distract, which is why they never hold on to long-term goals in life. Once they are gripped with an idea, a frustration or desire to do something, they throw all caution to the wind and proceed spontaneously to get what they want.

Never taking responsibility: When things go wrong in their plans, psychopaths never take the blame. It's always someone else's fault, and they make sure everybody knows it.

Fantastical view of self and life: Psychopaths always feel that they are "special" and that there are great things in store for them. They may suffer grandiose delusions about their self-worth, that they are kings or queens on their own private universe. They feel that they deserve only the best of everything—they won't settle for anything less, and they will do everything in their power to get what they want.

Seeking gratification and reward: There's nothing that matters more to a psychopath than personal gains and gratification, be it a desire for revenge against people who crossed him or a desire for monetary gain from his exploits.

Suicidal tendencies, often premeditated: Psychopaths often have a history of suicide attempts, not out of depression or low self-esteem, but probably as a way to seek attention or as a result of curiosity about how suicide works. Some may even use suicide threats to manipulate others (but they won't really make good on their threats).

Unreliable: You can't expect consistency from a psychopath; they have a tendency to miss even the most lenient deadlines. They forget to pay bills on time, skip out on meetings, and fail to show up to pre-arranged events. They're easily lured into doing things based on a whim, and they easily cave in to temptation. They're easily frustrated, which is why they rarely finish any projects or see anything through to its conclusion.

Lacking good sense and judgment: Psychopaths never learn from their mistakes. They insist on doing things their own way, even if their way has been proven to be wrong.

No long-term plans: Psychopaths are drifters with no definite plans for the future. They are unable to make lasting and long-term goals about what they plan to do with their lives, and thus frequently end up living nomadic lifestyles.

Jack of all crimes: Psychopaths are drawn to trying different criminal activities just to prove they can. This selection might range from simple crimes to complex and more heinous ones—theft or fraud to rape and murder.

Childhood and juvenile delinquency: Psychopathy may manifest itself as early as childhood. Children who had cases of extreme misbehavior, including theft, bullying, substance use and abuse, and vandalism are most likely to become psychopaths in the future. Teenagers who have been involved in any form of crime are also more prone to develop psychopathy, assuming they are not already suffering from the condition.

Psychopathy vs. Psychosis

Psychopaths are not the same as people who suffer from psychosis, neurosis, or psychiatric disorders like schizophrenia and other disorders with which fantasies and hallucinations are common. In fact, psychopaths usually have highly rational thought processes until the impulse to do something outrageous hits them.

Psychopaths don't have bouts of delusions or hallucinations wherein they can't distinguish reality from fantasy. They don't suffer from paranoia or any other psychiatric conditions (although, their bloated self-importance and egos may indicate a loss of touch with reality).

Just for Fun: The Psychopath Test—Are you one of them?

Here are the 20 traits of psychopathy according to the Hare PCL-R criteria. Give yourself a score of 0 if the characteristic does not apply to you at all, 1 if it slightly describes you, and 2 if it describes you perfectly.

Superficial charm – Are you a smooth-talker? Do you enjoy speaking in crowds, never getting tongue-tied or self-conscious? Do you speak your mind, no matter how it may affect others?

Rating: _____

Tremendous self-worth – Do you see yourself as very important? Do you believe you are superior above all other human beings? Have any of your friends (if you have any) told you that you're a tad too opinionated and overconfident at times?

Rating: _____

Tendency towards boredom – Do you hate routine? Do you crave excitement, taking risks, and doing dangerous tasks? Do you hate tedious tasks and often abandon projects mid-way because you've lost interest in them?

Rating: _____

Pathological lying – Do you think you're clever or shrewd? Do you possess a great deal of intelligence? Have you, in any instance, used your cleverness to deceive and control other people?

Rating: _____

Conning and manipulation – Do you use your skills of manipulation in order to cheat or exploit other people for personal gain? Have you ever been involved in or considered engaging in any form of fraudulent activity?

Rating: _____

Remorselessness – Do you feel nothing about the people that you've hurt or caused to suffer because of your schemes? Do you not sympathize with other people who have had bad things happen to them? Do you think anyone who's stupid enough to become your victim only deserves what they get?

Rating: _____

Shallow emotions – Do you often wonder what the fuss is all about when it comes to love and relationships? Have you never felt in love with someone, not even a modicum of affection? Do you hide your coldness and disconnect from others by maintaining a gregarious façade?

Rating: _____

Un-empathic and callous – Do you feel nothing about other people at all? Do you regard them all as useless unless you have a need for them? Do you not mind saying hurtful words to other people? Do you not consider the feelings of other people before you say or do something?

Rating: _____

Parasitic tendency – Do you prefer to live off others' works instead of doing hard work yourself? Do you intentionally manipulate others so that you can freeload off their hard-earned financial security? Would you rather get easy money from someone else than tax yourself in your career?

Rating: _____

Short temper – Are you easily annoyed or angered by the slightest mishap? Do you tend to show your anger or impatience easily? Do you resort to threats or even verbal and physical abuse when something or someone displeases you?

Rating: _____

Promiscuity – Have you had a lot of sexual partners? Have you ever maintained multiple relationships at the same time? Do you treat your partners coldly and almost impersonally, and regard sex only as a means to boost your ego?

Rating: _____

Aimlessness – Do you find it hard to develop long-term goals for yourself? Or, do you make plans but fail to follow through on them?

Rating: _____

Impulsivity – Do you tend to do things depending on your moods and whims? Are you easily tempted to try something that interests you and then plunge ahead without making any plans? Are you easily frustrated when things don't go your way?

Rating: _____

Childhood misbehavior – When you were a child, did you frequently get in trouble because of different misbehavior, such as lying, thievery, bullying, or vandalism? Have you ever run away from your home and family?

Rating: _____

Juvenile delinquency – When you were a teenager, did you have a record of criminal activity (convicted or otherwise)? Did you manipulate or bully other people, or engage in more serious crimes in your youth?

Rating: _____

Irresponsibility – Do you perpetually fail to keep your word and honor your promises to other people? Do you fail to meet deadlines and adhere to schedules simply because you can't push yourself to care about them?

Rating: _____

Laying blame on others – When things go wrong, do you have the tendency to immediately point a finger at other people? Do you think that your decisions are always right? Are you always on the defensive when people point out your mistakes? When you get blamed for something, do you respond by launching an antagonistic tirade that points the blame in an entirely new direction?

Rating: _____

Multiple failed marriages – Have you been married and divorced numerous times, or do you at least have several failed long-term relationships? Have your relationships failed because you couldn't commit to your partner long enough, and you ended up getting bored halfway through the relationship?

Rating: _____

Multiple crimes – Have you been engaged in different types of crimes? Do you pride yourself on your criminal activities? Have you committed any crimes that you got away with?

Rating: _____

Revocation of parole – Have you been in and out of jail numerous times? Have you reverted to criminal behavior, which resulted in the revocation of your parole?

Rating: _____

Scoring and Diagnostics

So, are you a psychopath or not? Psychopaths usually score 30 or above in the Hare-PCL-R diagnostic test, with 40 being the "perfect" stereotypical psychopath, while a "normal" individual with no psychopathic tendencies at all will score 5 or less. Non-psychopathic individuals with criminal backgrounds will likely have scores of around 22 and above, but no more than 30.

Another diagnostic tool is Cleckley's clinical profile for psychopathy, but the Hare PCL-R is the more widely used tool today.

CHAPTER 3

Personality Disorders and Psychopathy

Although psychopathy is not generally associated with psychosis or neurotic disorders, it is in fact considered to be the result of a personality disorder known as Anti-Social Personality Disorder, or APSD.

One of the tools for measuring and diagnosing APSD is the American Psychiatric Association (or APA's) Diagnostic and Statistical Manual of Mental Disorders (DSM), which helped create a common vocabulary and understanding of different psychological conditions and disorders.

However, diagnoses can be extremely difficult because of the inherent traits and behavioral patterns associated with psychopathy and APSD.

People with APSD are very good at deception; they usually appear normal at first glance. Some may lead double lives in order to satisfy their innate psychopathic tendencies while maintaining a sem-blance of respectability and social acclaim on the surface.

Because psychopathy is difficult to diagnose but often subject to public scrutiny, it's actually often confused with other personality disorders with which it shares similar symptoms and characteristics, like Narcissistic

Personality Disorder and Histrionic Personality Disorder.

Personality Disorders Associated with Psychopathy

Although APSD is the primary disorder that is linked with psychopathy, psychopathic individuals often also exhibit certain traits and characteristics exhibited by people who suffer from other personality disorders.

Known psychopaths often suffer from multiple personality disorders, which results in heightened psychopathic tendencies and antisocial behavior. There are also some disorders that may share similarities with APSD but are totally different from psychopathy, such as Borderline Personality Disorder.

Narcissistic Personality Disorder (NPD) refers to a mental condition wherein a person becomes excessively obsessed with him or herself in terms of physical looks, social prestige, and power, among other areas.

People afflicted with NPD usually suffer from grand delusions about their personal strengths, and because they hold themselves in high regard, they are also terribly ignorant of their shortcomings. They secretly envy others while harboring the illusion that others envy them.

Other terms for NPD are egocentrism and megalomania. People with NPD are in constant need of being praised and admired by others, but don't have the capacity to feel empathy for others.

Symptoms of NPD include arrogance, expectations of recognition and constant attention from other people, as well as delusions of grandeur about being extremely successful, intelligent, attractive, or powerful. NPD individuals also lack the ability to empathize with other people.

Borderline Personality Disorder (BPD) is often confused with psychopathy because both conditions cause individuals to behave impulsively and recklessly. However, whereas the psychopath suffers from emotional poverty, a person with BPD does things impulsively precisely because he or she is extremely emotionally sensitive to the stimulus and people around him or her.

People who commit crimes of passion and revenge may be suffering from BPD, but they are not considered to be psychopaths.

Psychopaths may experience any of these disorders alongside ASPD, in addition to other anxiety disorders, depressive disorders, and even substance abuse. Having multiple disorders usually amplifies the psychopathic traits and characteristics of a psychopathic individual.

Histrionic Personality Disorder is an attention-seeking disorder that is usually driven by low self-esteem. People with HPD often engage in risqué behavior and seek constant approval. They are also extremely sensitive to negative comments and criticism from other people.

HPD is similar to psychopathy in terms of seeking attention, apparent egoism, risky decision-making, deception, and easy frustration. Those with HPD are also socially successful and tend to use their social skills to manipulate others. The gross difference between HPD and psychopathy is that people with HPD are very emotional, which is in fact the driving force behind their attention-seeking behavior.

Of all psychological disorders, ASPD is the one most commonly linked to psychopathy. It is distinguishable from all other disorders because its symptoms mostly match the criteria for psychopathy as outlined by Cleckley himself.

ASPD Definition

ASPD (also known as Dissocial Personality Disorder) refers to a personality disorder wherein an individual repeatedly engages in antisocial behavior without any regard for other people's rights and general welfare. People with ASPD often have poor senses of morality and affection, as well as a long history of aggressive and criminal behavior, sometimes beginning from childhood.

Under the APA-DSM 4th edition, ASPD is clustered with other personality disorders characterized by erratic behavioral patterns (Axis II-Cluster B).

ASPD Symptoms

The APA bases its diagnosis of ASPD on the following behaviors and characteristics:

1.) Constant disregard for social norms and the violation of legal rights of others, usually dating back to teenage years

2.) Habitual or pathological lying, to the point of deceiving others for personal gain

3.) Always acting upon impulse and having the inability to make any plans for the future

4.) Aggression and quick temper, manifested in frequent cases of engaging in physical brawls or assaults against other people

5.) Perpetual failure to honor promises and obligations

6.) Lack of empathy for others and an inability to feel remorse for antisocial behavior which has harmed other people—sometimes even defending antisocial acts by rationalizing them

ASPD is only diagnosed in people of legal age (over 18 years), although experts usually look for early symptoms such as perpetual misbehavior during childhood. Experts also rule out other psychotic disorders by ensuring that episodes of antisocial behavior occur when the patient is in a rational state and not during bouts of hallucinations associated with schizophrenia or manic-depressive episodes.

ASPD and Psychopathy

Although ASPD is often linked to the diagnosis of psychopathy, there remains a controversy among psychological experts regarding the correlation of these two conditions.

Some experts argue that these conditions are synonymous to each other, but some say that they are different because they are diagnosed differently (the Hare PCL-R for psychopathy and the APA DSM-IV for ASPD). ASPD diagnoses focus more on behavioral patterns, while in diagnosing psychopathy, an individual's self-perception and the subjective judgment of one's traits are relied upon.

For the purposes of this book, we will refer to ASPD and psychopathy as similar concepts, often used in conjunction with each other. These terms are often used interchangeably, and in court cases, both are used to countercheck any related diagnosis.

ASPD Subtypes

Another component of diagnosing ASPD is categorization. Given the surrounding controversies regarding psychopathy and ASPD, another expert, Thomas Millon, devised several subtypes to classify ASPD patients according to their dominant behavioral tendencies or patterns.

Nomadic ASPD: Nomadic ASPD patients have dominant avoidant and schizoid traits; they often feel that their lives are comprised of nothing but a streak of bad luck. These are the drifter psychopaths who live on the fringes of society as vagrants, misfits, school dropouts, and tramps. These people are generally malevolent and suspicious of other people.

Malevolent ASPD: Possibly one of the most dangerous subtypes, psychopaths who fall into this category have dominant tendencies related to sadism and paranoia. They are vicious and belligerent by nature, with short tempers and a thirst for revenge. They don't feel guilt or fear, and they are very suspicious of all people in general, even their friends and family. These psychopaths often expect to be betrayed by others. They tend to lash out through extremely violent and vicious acts.

Covetous/Psychopathic ASPD: This is one subtype of APSD that exhibits a somewhat "pure" form of psychopathy, because people who fall into this subtype are often motivated to commit crimes due to greed or envy of other people's possessions and good fortune. They feel deprived and are always discontented with what they have—they take more pleasure in taking something away from others rather than the actual act of possession.

Risk-taking ASPD: Psychopaths who fall into this subtype display traits related to HPD, which makes them crave danger and do things impulsively. Fearless and reckless, these individuals mostly commit crimes for the sake of thrills and the excitement of getting caught.

Narcissistic ASPD: These psychopaths are self-centered individuals who usually lead respectable lives on the surface. Some of them are even leaders of the community, highly-regarded and respected in their careers. They commit psychopathic crimes in secret, and when discovered, their first impulse is to defend their reputations. Their inherent need to be considered formidable and invincible is their most dominant behavior characteristic.

ASPD Causes

As with other psychological conditions, ASPD is often the result of a confluence of factors, both genetic/biological and psycho-social. Psychological experts claim that genetics is the primary factor in play with psychopathy, although traumatic events may be the triggers.

Neuro-scientists also claim that there is a direct correlation between the incidence of ASPD and lowered serotonin levels. Serotonin is a feel-good hormone released from the human brain that is responsible for intensifying feelings of happiness and other emotional highs.

According to experts, the malformation of certain parts of the brain as well as the physical effects of alcoholism and substance abuse are also possible factors. Traumatic brain injury is also related to some extent, since this can affect a person's ability to understand and follow moral and social norms.

However, psychologists also stress the importance of socio-cultural factors in increasing the chances of developing ASPD or psychopathy. Children may be affected by parents who exhibit psychopathic traits themselves, as well as by how the surrounding communities view and respond to misbehavior in children and teenagers.

ASPD Therapy and Treatment

One common misconception about ASPD and psychopathy is that they cannot be treated. While it is true that ASPD is difficult to treat, it is not impossible; recent groundbreaking Dutch research suggests that some psychopaths are not completely devoid of emotions—they are just able to turn their emotions on and off at whim.

What makes therapy especially difficult for psychopaths is their inability to feel remorse and guilt; because they don't feel empathy, they also don't understand the costs of their antisocial behavior for their victims. In some cases, psychopaths even simulate expressions of remorse just to make it appear that the therapy is working.

Treatment is still possible with the proper care and administration of a professional, but an external force is required to ensure that the psychopath adheres to routine therapy. Psychopaths won't be motivated to undergo therapy voluntarily because they don't see any way they can gain from it.

Empathy and Psychopathy

This is the most telling and basic symptom of psychopathy: shallowness of emotion or a complete lack of emotions, a cold disdain and disregard for other people, including their rights, welfare, and interests.

Whether it's genetic or as a result of an abusive childhood, all psychopaths have no capacity to feel love for others or to feel any form of affection. Some might understand social norms and definitions of emotions enough to simulate them—but often this understanding is used and abused to manipulate and control others.

Psychopaths don't feel remorse for their actions either, because they've never experienced a sense of loss themselves. This is why many convicted serial killers never show any signs of guilt or remorse even to the very end, and their only regrets are usually self-centered ones about being caught or having destroyed their reputations.

Narcissism and Psychopathy

Not all psychopaths are dominantly narcissistic, but most exhibit a substantial amount of megalomania. They are too self-absorbed in their wants, needs and desires, often to the point that they manage to construct fantastical views of themselves and their accomplishments. Often, narcissism comes into the fore during the actual performance of antisocial acts (such as murder).

Fear and Psychopathy

Psychopaths are reckless and impulsive because they do not feel fear, even in the face of death. However, they do understand the concept of fear, and they often put it to use to humiliate and debase their victims.

Fear is one of the best tools of a psychopath, along with pain, and many cultural references and over-hyped images of psychopathy in the media only work to the advantage of psychopaths.

Anger and Psychopathy

There is some debate whether psychopaths are able to experience anger. Although many psychopaths may have short tempers and poor behavioral controls, experts suggest that criminal psychopaths don't really feel anger during their worst crimes.

However, they believe that psychopaths do have feelings of repressed anger, which manifest in the acts of violence that they commit, whether consciously or not.

Violence and Psychopathy

Psychopathy almost always leads to some form of violence, whether physical, verbal, or worse. This is the only language that the worst psychopaths understand and enjoy: making other people submit to their whims through acts of violence.

For them, violence may be an empowering act, or it may be a manifestation of their subconscious need to seek revenge against someone who has hurt or offended them in the past.

CHAPTER 4

Crime and Psychopaths

Not all psychopaths are criminals, and not all criminals are psychopaths. However, psychopaths are more prone to becoming criminals when they are given opportunities where they can get away with crimes. Their manipulative skills and charming exteriors make all psychopaths the most dangerous kind of criminals and potential criminals.

Criminal Minds Explained

Research suggests that there are some neurological bases for psychopathy. In a controlled clinical study of a group of convicted psychopaths and another group of ordinary individuals, brain scans showed that the former had a smaller middle-frontal and orbital-frontal gyri compared to the control group.

Researchers also discovered that many psychopaths had deformities in the amygdala, the portion of the brain associated with emotions. This explains why true psychopaths are incapable of feeling emotions like empathy, guilt, and love.

Aside from neurological factors, early childhood experiences, adult models, and criminal imprisonment are all possible situations that might trigger or aggravate an individual's psychopathic tendencies.

Childhood Maldevelopment

Experts suggest that psychopaths are incapable of forming lasting attachments and instead create only superficial power-play relationships (often sado-masochistic in nature) wherein they have control over their partners. This can be rooted back to their early childhood, often as a result of having an abusive and aggressive parent or guardian as a role model.

Psychologists explain that eventually, a psychopathic child experiences a split into two personas: the vulnerable child subjected to abuse, and the external personality that serves as armoured protection the inner child. Because the child thinks that any interaction with his environment will be painful, he chooses to isolate himself inside and views everyone else as a potential threat to his safety and security.

The Teen Psychopath

Once a child reaches teenage years without a change in the negative factors in his environment, the threat that he will develop into a psychopath in adulthood multiplies tenfold.

An abused child may become exposed to the wrong kind of peers when he reaches his teens, or he may become even more isolated and misunderstood. In either case, the psychopathic tendencies that began to take root during childhood may intensify, and the adolescent will soon move on to more serious acts of cruelty and callousness.

Juvenile delinquency is the next step down the road for a psychopath in the making. Whether they get caught or not, psychopaths usually have a history of criminal activities during their teenage years: vandalism, bullying, animal cruelty, alcohol use, and even cases of arson and other serious offences.

The Full-Grown Psychopath

A full-grown psychopath is a force to be reckoned with. Although not all psychopaths are a danger to society, many of them are in fact dangerous when crossed, even ones that are not criminally inclined.

Psychopaths view potential victims not as people, but as mere symbols and representations of something that they desire and wish to own. Some psychopathic criminals tend to go into a haze during their acts of violence. They do not feel anger towards their victims, but it is the obvious message communicated by the horrific acts they commit, whether or not they are aware of it.

Some psychopaths also undergo episodes of hallucinations while partaking in antisocial acts. They are often drawn into images of mythical heroes and imagine themselves as such during their most horrendous crimes.

Although all convicted psychopathic criminals undergo therapy sessions in exchange for parole, some experts say that there are psychopaths who are beyond redemption. These are the ones who can carry out an entire plot of deception by reading books on psychology and psychopathy and using their newfound knowledge to manipulate the people who are handling their therapy sessions into believing that they have been treated.

Some psychopaths even go so far as to pretend to have another mental disorder that is more prone to eliciting sympathy (such as schizophrenia and other disorders related to psychosis) just to avoid being diagnosed with ASPD or psychopathy.

In fact, some of the worst psychopaths have been cleared several times for parole, only to revert to their criminal acts and be caught again. They charm and talk their way out of prison, only to go back to their criminal behavior. Some even plead criminal insanity and psychosis just to get away from taking responsibility for their actions.

Criminal Profiling: Regular Criminals vs. Psychopaths

In the previous chapters, we covered the different tools used by psychiatric experts and criminologists to diagnose psychopathy in convicted criminals. For two-bit criminals whose only claims to fame are fraudulent acts and conning, finding the psychopathic diagnosis doesn't seem so important, but when it comes to those who have committed heinous acts, it is essential.

A diagnosis of psychopathy can cause complications in the legalities of the criminal judicial process, especially when horrendous crimes are involved. There are three primary types of psychopathic criminals who fall into the category of the worst kinds of criminals in existence:

Serial killers are psychopaths who often target victims of a specific demographic (female/male, of a certain age, or physical appearance), assault them sexually, and torture or beat them to death. Some serial killers, like Ted Bundy, also commit perverted sexual acts like necrophilia, as a final debasement and humiliation of their victims. Serial killers are often sadists who have morbid fantasies and a compulsion to kill.

Mass murderers are psychopaths who seem normal, but one day, they snap and kill a large number of people at once. One of the more recent examples of this is the teenager responsible for the Virginia Tech massacre.

Spree killers are psychopaths who kill different people in numerous locations in a matter of hours, days, or weeks. There is always at least one similarity in the way the victims are killed, almost as if the psychopath wants to leave clues to help authorities discover his identity.

World's Worst Historic Psychopaths

Again, not all psychopaths are criminals, but the most notorious and fascinating psychopaths often are criminals. The rest of the pack does not attract the attention of ordinary, non-psychopathic people, because they keep a low profile. The only fascination you might have with unidentified psychopaths is the possibility that you actually are acquainted with one.

So, as a final offering, this chapter presents the worst psychopaths that have ever walked the earth, along with a brief profile and list of horrendous crimes.

Albert Fish: If you've watched Silence of the Lambs, then you're probably acquainted with Hannibal Lecter. Albert Fish is the real version of Hannibal Lecter, only much worse, and very much twisted. He is also known throughout history as the Gray Man, the Brooklyn Vampire, and the Werewolf of Wysteria.

Albert Fish was a cannibal, serial killer, and child molester. His favorite victims were young children of both sexes, whom he enticed to come with him by offering treats to them. He would molest them first, then kill them and dismember them before eating them.

To add insult to injury, Fish's signature act was to send letters to the families of his child victims, detailing how he molested, killed, and ate them. Fish had about a dozen other sexual perversions aside from cannibalism, including coprophilia (arousal from eating fecal matter) and necrophilia.

Fish was ruled to have been criminally insane, supposedly due to genetic anomalies, as his parents were close relatives of each other. He was sentenced to electrocution, a prospect which actually fascinated him to the end.

Jack the Ripper: The case of Jack the Ripper case is probably one of the world's greatest unsolved criminal cases. Jack the Ripper was an anonymous serial killer who preyed upon the prostitutes of London in the late 1800s. His signature method of killing was to slit the throats of his victims, thus earning him the moniker Jack the Ripper.

There are many conspiracy theories linking Jack the Ripper to other psychopathic criminals during that time, but there was never enough evidence to link him to anyone of them.

Adolf Hitler: There have been some studies that suggest the correlation of psychopathy with people in high levels of authority in government. Adolf Hitler is one of the glaring examples that can be used to support this claim. Hitler is best known for megalomania, which was inherent in his belief that the German race is superior to others. He is also responsible for the genocide of many Jews who lived in Germany and other countries during his rule, as well as inhumane concentration camps and other forms of torture.

John Wayne Gacy Jr., the Killer Clown: John Wayne Gacy Jr. was a convicted serial rapist and murderer of men and young boys. He was responsible for the deaths of no less than 33 people in between 1972 and 1978. The nickname "Killer Clown" comes from his occupation as a clown entertainer in children's parties.

Jeffrey Dahmer, the Milwaukee Cannibal: In a span of almost two decades, from 1978 to 1991, Jeffrey Dahmer murdered at least 20 men. But that's not the most heinous of his crimes: he had an occult obsession with the corpses of his victims. He was caught because his apartment began to smell of rotting flesh, and authorities soon discovered severed heads and corpses inside his fridge and in large containers. There was proof that he had sex with his victims' corpses and that he also engaged in cannibalism.

He was convicted to 15 life sentences, but his time was cut short when he was beaten to death by a fellow inmate in 1994.

CHAPTER 5

Psychopaths vs. Sociopaths

Another modern term for psychopath is sociopath, but experts say there is a distinct difference between individuals who fall on these two categories. Ordinary people often use these terms inter-changeably, but similar to the case of ASPD and psychopathy, there is some dispute regarding the synonymity of these two terms.

Some experts claim that sociopathy and psychopathy are two different strands (or subtypes) of APSD, with major differences in terms of dominant behavioural traits and patterns. Also, while psychopathy is said to be caused primarily by genetic factors, sociopathy is said to be the result of psycho-social and environ-mental ones.

Following this line of argument, here is a clarification of the subtle but distinct differences between these two conditions.

Delineating Psychopaths and Sociopaths

Psychopaths are those people who are said to be born with genetic anomalies or maldeveloped parts of their central nervous system. This results to a heightened impulsivity and recklessness, as well as emotional poverty and inability to process socially accepted norms and behaviour.

In contrast, sociopaths are people who have normal biological makeup but still exhibit psychopathic/ antisocial behavioural patterns. These individuals tend to develop ASPD more as a result of negative psycho-social factors in their environment, including but not limited to familial neglect, choosing the "wrong" kinds of friends, and poverty or social standing.

For psychiatrists, these two strands of ASPD are more or less the same, and often psychopaths and sociopaths are subject to similar therapy and treatment. However, in the field of criminology and law and order, experts choose to distinguish between the two and have different ways of handling them.

According to criminologists, a psychopath is highly impulsive and without conscience, while sociopaths are not necessarily always impulsive. Psychopaths are also more erratic and difficult to second-guess, while a sociopath exhibits strong controls over their behaviour.

Psychopaths often get caught because of their impulsivity and recklessness—they tend to leave clues behind after they commit a crime (both intentionally or oversight). On the other hand, sociopaths are very crafty when it comes to pre-meditated crimes—they only take risks when the chances are high that they won't get caught. They cover their tracks to avoid being traced.

Psychopaths are more known for excessively impulsive criminal tendencies. They are opportunistic criminals, which mean that they will strike whenever there is a chance to cheat, con, or victimize other people, often without a second thought to the possible risks. This is contradictory for the cautious sociopath, who only strikes in a situation or environment where he can be in control. In some cases, sociopaths can even plan to commit crimes years ahead, carefully laying out their plans for a particular target.

In terms of relationships, psychopaths are those who don't seem able to commit to long-term relationships, as evidenced by their numerous failed marriages or partnerships of any sort. Sociopaths, meanwhile, try to maintain a façade of normalcy when it comes to relationships. In fact, sociopaths often use their mask of affluence to prey on unsuspecting victims.

Sociopaths are able to maintain stable careers, because they are highly-organized individuals as opposed to the clutter-brained, easily distractible psychopath. In some ways, sociopaths have a level of understanding when it comes to human affections and emotions, they just don't have the capacity to feel and experience them firsthand.

Lastly, psychopaths are highly violent, while sociopaths are not necessarily predisposed to commit violent acts.

Similarities of Psychopaths and Sociopaths

Despite their distinct differences, there are also numerous similarities in terms of behavioural tendencies between psychopaths and sociopaths. For one, they both don't care anything at all about the welfare and rights of other people, which make them capable of doing almost anything.

Both psychopaths and sociopaths have early manifestations of cruelty and misbehaviour, even criminal activities, sometimes as early as childhood or during mid-teens. These are not singular cases or instances, but often repetitive patterns without any signs of remorse.

Both strands of APSD, psychopathy and sociopathy, tend to result to violent antisocial crimes. However, in this light, sociopaths appear to be more sinister than psychopaths because of their capacity to mask their psychopathic tendencies underneath being a high-functioning, charming and legitimate member of society.

What's even more daunting is the statistical information that both criminally-inclined psychopaths and sociopaths are more persuasive than non-psychopathic criminals. As a result, they tend to get released from prison much quicker than regular criminals.

Blurred Lines of Distinction

The differentiation of psychopaths and sociopaths are still subject to varied interpretations, even among experts. One case of psychopathy may be entirely different to another one.

What's important is to understand the innate traits and characteristics associated with both psychopathy and sociopathy. Distinctions will hardly matter when you become a target of either one of them.

Historical Sociopath: Ted Bundy

According to the working definition provided in this chapter, it can be agreed upon that sociopaths are somewhat more dangerous than your average psychopath. In fact, some of the most historical criminals who have been dubbed as psychopaths actually led normal lives before their crimes caught up with them. Some are even highly-regarded members of their communities with successful careers.

One of the most popular examples of a sociopath is the serial rapist-murderer Ted Bundy, who was convicted for at least 30 counts of rape-slay cases.

Before he was caught for his crimes, Ted Bundy was considered an excellent young man who was in his final years of law school. He had a brilliant political career ahead of him, and all of his acquaintances thought that he was a likeable and charming fellow.

However, beneath all that glossy charm, Bundy was living a double life. During a brief period before the series of rape-slay murders began, he was dating two women at the same time. His accounts of his early childhood and family background during the course of his trial and eventual conviction are also contradictory, so it is uncertain whether he had been exposed to a grandfather who had psychopathic tendencies or not.

At the height of the murders, Bundy began showing signs of irresponsibility, until he completely dropped out of law school, surprising his acquaintances.

The crimes: Ted Bundy is best known as a serial rapist and murderer of at least 30 women or more, but what many people don't know are the specifics of those crimes.

In essence, Bundy was a sadistic and violent killer who beat and strangled his victims to death—but that wasn't the worst of his crimes. He was also a necrophile: after committing his crimes, he returns to the crime scene to have sex with the corpses repeatedly. For Bundy, women were merely toys he targeted and played with.

To the end of his trial, he never admitted to the charges against him despite the overwhelming evidence to the contrary. He was a pathological liar, and he showed no remorse to the very end—his only regret was that he was careless enough to get caught.

Although he did confess to his crimes in some interviews, he withdrew them as he walked towards his death, claiming that those were only desperate pleas and that they weren't true.

CHAPTER 6

Sociopathy Defined

Sociopaths are often viewed with extreme prejudice and are often treated as a threat. That is because most people are stuck with the thinking that sociopaths are criminals, serial killers, and generally dangerous people. But, the truth is that most sociopaths live among us and they seem to live normal lives.

The Common Characteristics of Sociopaths

One of the first things you should know about sociopaths is that they can be very charming. These are people who are equipped with charisma. This is one of the main characteristics of a sociopath that allows them to draw people in. The glow in their personality gives other people the impression that they can be trusted. Other people tend to go to them for guidance and direction.

Sociopaths have an innocent charisma. But, they are also gifted with sexual appeal, although this does not mean that all sexy people are sociopaths. The sexual appetite of the typical sociopath is rather over the top. They are also likely to have weird fetishes.

As compared to other people, sociopaths are rather spontaneous. They can be very intense, which at times can be mistaken for passion. They are bizarre and are more likely to be erratic. While most people act within the normal social norms and respect social contracts, sociopaths are wary about such things. They are likely to behave in an irrational manner. They often engage in risky behavior.

The feelings of guilt, remorse, and shame are some things that normal people are quite familiar with. A sociopath, on the other hand, lacks these feelings. Their brains that lack the proper circuitry that is capable of processing these emotions.

For this reason, sociopaths find it easy to betray other people. They also find it "normal" to resort to threats. They can even harm others. When they have their mind set on something, they are unlikely to be swayed.

Sociopaths are self serving. Their main concern is their own interests. It does not matter whether they harm people along the way, as long as they get what they want, when they want it. Some people who serve in government positions have this kind of tendency. To them, the end justifies the means.

Sociopaths are likely to be liars. They are in fact, pathological liars. They have no problem inventing truth. They lie about everything, including their experiences. They also exaggerate. They do so to the point of absurdity. But, because they have a gift for storytelling, they are rather believable.

Sociopaths can win people over. They are fixated on the idea of winning. They will not back down in an argument or a fight. Sociopaths will defend their stories and lies viciously. They will do whatever it takes to avoid getting caught in their own web of lies.

These are considered to be highly intelligent people. The problem is, they often use their intelligence for deception. For a sociopath, being able to deceive others gives them some kind of power.

Sociopaths are likely to have high IQs. While this may be a positive thing, the way they decide to use their intelligence is what makes them dangerous. This is proven by those sociopathic serial killers who can evade law enforcement.

Sociopaths are self centered. They do not feel love the way other people do. They lack love and compassion. However, they can fake these emotions in an effort to get what they want and what they think they deserve.

These people also have a gift for words. They speak poetically. Sociopaths are master wordsmiths. Their monologues and speeches can be very hypnotic, and the same time, very intriguing. They are   excellent storytellers.

Sociopaths will never apologize for the things they do wrong. They will never admit to any faults. That is because in their minds, they lack such awareness. They feel no guilt and they have no conscience to bother them.

Even if they are confronted with strong evidence, a sociopath will find a way to escape being confronted. Instead of apologizing, a sociopath will resort to an attack that makes the other person feel guilty. They can turn the tables, just like that.

What makes the lies of a sociopath believable is the fact that they believe their own lies. A sociopath can twist the truth with his or her words. They are outstanding at creating illusions.

How to get to the truth?

Sociopaths can create their own truth. They are experts in creating elaborate stories and fictional explanations in an effort to justify their actions. They create illusions.

When a sociopath is caught red-handed, he will deny his guilt and never apologize. Rather, a sociopath will respond with threats and   anger. He will then create new lies and invent a more elaborate explanation to get away from being held responsible for what he was caught doing.

For instance, a sociopath who has just been caught with stolen bag full of cash will never admit that he actually stole the money. Instead, he is likely to deny the truth. He would invent a story, for instance, that he is actually saving the money to prevent other people from stealing it. He might say he is trying to give the money back to the rightful owner.

If you did not know any better, you would believe the story and actually declare the thief a hero. Someone who questions the sociopath will be met with an attack. The sociopath is more likely to defend his "honor" and shame you for even questioning his so called honesty.

The lack of conscience, shame, remorse, and guilt makes the sociopath's mind a truly criminal one. The way a sociopath's mind works is perfect for committing and getting away with crimes. They can deceive people, creating arguments and strife. They can make people turn against each other. Sociopaths are extremely delusional. While they may be intelligent, they can defy logical reasoning.

It can be very difficult and even impossible to reason with a sociopath. If you want to find out the truth, you have to ask questions, but you must proceed with caution. Otherwise, you will only drown further in the sociopath's ocean of lies. You should never attempt to reason with this kind of person, unless you want to waste your time. Reasoning with a sociopath will only cause you to annoy him. Trying to reason with this kind of individual is essentially a futile cause.

CHAPTER 7

The Goal of a Sociopath

Sociopaths are often associated with serial killers. While there are many serial killers who are diagnosed sociopaths, some sociopaths are capable of living ordinary lives. What makes them different is that while they may lead seemingly normal lives, they do things differently.

These people lack conscience. They are not capable of feeling affection. Essentially, they do not have a care about other people, including those close to them, those people who they are supposed to care for.

Sociopaths do not feel empathy. They do not feel the same emotions as the rest of the population, but they can be very good observers. Their skills of observation allow them to mimic affection and empathy. This also makes it challenging to detect them.

Undetected, sociopaths can ruin their families, their supposed friends, and the people they work with. A sociopath is a master of deception. These people would take whatever it is they want even if it means hurting other people, especially those that will get in the way. And, they never feel sorry. They manipulate and lie to people without a second thought. They can leave other people confused and ruined.

While some studies confirm the early warning signs of sociopathy, research is still unable to determine the link between this condition and the kind of childhood a sociopath has. That means a sociopath may come from any kind of family or from any kind of childhood.

What is certain, however, is that a sociopath's brain functions differently as compared to a normal brain. A sociopath's brain works in such a way that the emotional life is unusually shallow. But, through observation, they can copy emotions and make it believable, just like a professional actor can.

What Do Sociopaths Want?

A normal person's purpose is most likely driven by affections and connections with other people. For a normal person, loving relationships with other individuals ultimately lend meaning to life. A sociopath does not feel the same emotions. So, what is it that influences a sociopath's purpose? What is a sociopath's purpose? What is it that they want?

Top Things a Sociopath Wants

A sociopath is most likely to target someone who has what he wants or has something that can help him get what he wants. Most of the time, it is about money. But, that is not always the case. In addition to money, here is a list of the top things a sociopath may want.

Sex

It is easy to bore a sociopath. This is why they will always crave stimulation. As such, they turn to what they find highly stimulating: that is, sex. For this reason, sociopaths are more likely to have multiple sexual affairs at the same time. And, this is why their relationships do not usually last.

However, sociopaths are far different from sex addicts. They are not enslaved by the need for sex. Rather, they merely use sex to cure boredom. They also use sex as a vital tool of manipulation. They use sex and the person involved to get what they want.

Housing

What makes sociopaths most effective at manipulation is that they do not directly ask for what they want. Instead, they can make people voluntarily hand it to them. For instance, a sociopath who needs money will not directly ask for it. Rather, he may insinuate that he wants to live with his partner/victim. Making this suggestion will make the other person feel loved and wanted. A sociopath will want the other person to feel this way. But, the truth is, the sociopath merely has nowhere else to go.

Services

There are chores that we do not really like doing. In most cases, we do them ourselves anyway, or pay someone to do it on our behalf. But, a sociopath will not take that route. Rather, he will use someone to do it for him. A sociopath is more likely to engage in a relationship to make his life much easier and more comfortable so he does not have to do the things he does not want like cleaning, cooking, or even taking care of children.

Status

Someone can guess at your character by taking a look at the people you hang out with. But, for most normal people, association with the rich and famous is not enough to make them want a personal connection. For a sociopath, however, wealth, fame, and success may be far more important that affection, simply because they do not feel any. A sociopath is likely to form a seemingly real relationship with another person for the sole purpose of improving his status.

Entertainment

A sociopath gets easily bored. Excitement and stimulation is what he craves. This is also why sociopaths are more likely to seek out people who have access to an exciting social scene. They may use other people to form connections with personalities who can give them a taste of excitement.

Connections

Connections are indeed important for success. A sociopath is well aware of that. The problem is, they do not recognize any boundaries. As such, they do not hesitate to use someone who has connections or has the skills to help them reach their goals.

Image

Image is very important to a sociopath, as it is to everyone else. A sociopath knows he is different from everyone else, and the last thing he wants is to be discovered. In order to hide his true nature, a sociopath will build a very specific image of himself to present to the world. And, he will stop at nothing to complete and protect it, even if it means using someone or hurting another person's feelings.

Cover

A sociopath always has a hidden agenda. Because he is concerned about protecting his image so that he will not be detected, a sociopath is likely to live a double life. A sociopath will use other people as cover so that his hidden agenda will not be discovered. This way, he can   operate as he pleases and get what he wants without being found out.

Fun

Because normal people have empathy, the idea of using other individuals for fun is not appealing. A sociopath, however, free from empathy and having no regard for social norms, does not hesitate about using, manipulating, and deceiving other people just because he can. A sociopath may do things just for fun.

Sociopaths like the idea of being above everyone else. It gives them the pleasure of being in control. They may seduce and break other people's hearts because it gives them delight.

Domination

Power and control are two of the main driving forces of sociopaths. They will pursue domination to feed their need for feeling superior. In their minds, they are more powerful, smarter, and more capable than others. And, they will prove it, even if it means destroying other lives along the way.

A sociopath wants to WIN!

Ultimately, a sociopath is driven by the want to win. The ultimate goal is winning, and a sociopath is ready to do anything at all and employ any means for the sake of winning.

They do not care about love and relationships like most people do. Without such factors as part of the equation, what feels important to them is merely winning—winning at all costs and winning the game, whatever game it is they are currently preoccupied with.

For instance, winning, for a sociopath who is in business, may be to get rich and eliminate the competition. For a sociopath who is caught up in a sibling rivalry, winning would be to defeat the sibling. Winning for a sociopath can also mean making other people suffer, lose, or fail. Winning could mean doing whatever it takes to cause the embarrassment, frustration, and demise of other people.

Sociopaths are conniving and clever. That's because unlike normal people, they do not have a lot to think about. They have no regard for morals and no concern for relationships. They are not bound by conflicting feelings. This allows them to think of more effective ways to earn the trust of people, only to stab them in the back. They manipulate and deceive, and the people they are using either have no idea what is going on or choose to deny the truth.

Normal people do not usually feel burdened by boredom, because relationships with other people keep them busy. Since a sociopath could care less about such things, their interest shifts to preventing boredom instead. For a normal person, boredom is much more tolerable than worry, upset, drama, and other negative emotions. But, for a sociopath, boredom is the most intolerable of all. This is where their incessant urge for stimulation comes from. Playing the game to win keeps them busy, interested, and occupied.

Sociopaths are very different from normal people. It makes them difficult to understand and troubling to deal with. Their lack of empathy itself may be incomprehensible to a lot of people.

CHAPTER 8

The Weaknesses of a Sociopath

Sociopaths are wired differently. It is just not a matter of upbringing that makes them so different. Their inability and incapacity to feel emotions just like normal people do is something that is deeply embedded in their being.

Fear may be normal to a lot of people, but it is not something that sociopaths have much of. Somehow, this also puts them in a powerful position.

Sociopaths can easily spot the weaknesses of other people. They use such information to manipulate. It is easy for them because they essentially do not care about other people. They do not care about anybody else but themselves. However, sociopaths do have their own share of fears. These fears may be different from what normal people fear. Nevertheless, sociopaths are afraid of two things.

Two Things that Sociopaths Fear

There are basically two things that sociopaths fear. One is the fear of losing control, and the other is the fear of being exposed.

Their sense of purpose is driven not by love and relationships. Rather, they are driven by power and control. And, their biggest fear is losing both.

Sociopaths fear losing control.

There are people who have the constant urge to be in control of things. But, a sociopath's need for control is much more different. They don't just want to control everything; they also need to be in control of everyone. And, they have a clever way of hiding this need of control.

Some people are transparent. You can easily tell whether or not they have obsessive compulsive tendencies. Sociopaths operate differently. They project a different image. They make themselves seem like laid back and relaxed individuals, making it so easy to trust them that a normal person will never suspect them.

Sociopaths hide their desire for control. And, most people who come across sociopaths are quite clueless about being controlled. When a sociopath loses this advantage, when a sociopath loses control, he will break down. A sociopath is well aware of this, which is why he will do anything to keep control of things and of people.

Sociopaths fear being exposed.

A sociopath is quite aware that he is different. He knows he is unlike normal people. And, he is afraid of being exposed. This is why he builds an image, pretends, and protects his status so that he will remain undetected. He seeks cover, and it does not matter who he uses to keep that cover.

Lying, deception, and manipulation is what a sociopath resorts to. He can be very creative and resourceful when it comes to hiding his true self. He is willing to go to great lengths to keep people from finding out the real person he is behind the mask he carefully wears.

This is why sociopaths cling on to people they have used. They do not like ending relationships, although they know they are hurting and ruining the other person. When a sociopath refuses to break up with a lover, it does not mean that he cannot live without the person or that he truly cares. His refusal to let go stems from his fear of losing control over the other person and the fear of being exposed.

What are the things that a sociopath will do to prevent losing control and being exposed?

A sociopath is more likely to instil fear in his partner. This can make the other person afraid of exposing the sociopath. The risk is still present, though, which is why the sociopath will take precautions. To ensure that he will not be exposed, he will destroy the other person's credibility. He will spread lies and make the other person look bad to the point of insanity. This makes the sociopath sure that when the other person talks ill of him, no one will believe it.

A sociopath will make threats. He will stalk and harass people who may know about the real person inside. It does not matter how long the relationship has lasted or how deeply invested the other person is. A sociopath only truly cares about himself and his own needs, and he will protect himself at all costs, even if it means harming others in the process. Needless to say, engaging in relationship with a sociopath is destructive.

Why is a sociopath afraid of losing control?

Control is one of the essential things that keep a sociopath focused. His goals and life plan are driven by the desire for control. He does not value love or relationships. Power and control are the only things that give value to his life. Take those away, and the sociopath will be reduced to nothing.

A sociopath sees other people only as sources of supply or as tools. A sociopath may fear losing a loved one. But, it is not because he cares for the other person. It is merely because he fears losing his source of supply.

In a romantic relationship, the sociopath will do anything and say   everything to keep the other person attached. To be able to have   control over his own life, the sociopath feels the need to keep controlling the other person, as well as others.

A sociopath may feel paranoid, possessive, and jealous. But, underneath those feelings is ultimately the fear of losing control over someone they own. A sociopath never views someone he is romantically involved with as partner. Rather, he sees the other person as a possession.

Why is a sociopath afraid of being exposed?

Sociopaths are incredibly charming. People are attracted to them because of their charisma. People readily accept and trust sociopaths. They use their gift of charm to win people over. This also makes it easy for them to manipulate and deceive people.

Sociopaths create an illusion, a false image that draws people in, who eventually become their victims. The sociopath wants to prevent exposure. This is why a sociopath wants to keep his sources of supply close and under control. Otherwise, he will draw suspicion, and that will make it much more difficult for him to manipulate other people.

A sociopath is drawn to the easy kind of life. He likes to be handed things for free. He likes to live off of others. He feels entitled, and so he makes other people work for him. If he feels in any way threatened, he will stop at nothing to eliminate said threat.

For these reasons, it would be foolish to attempt to expose a sociopath. A normal person cannot beat a sociopath at his own game. Any such attempts may only backfire. For one, a sociopath is capable of things that a normal person will not even dare to think of doing. Therefore, it would be wiser to walk away as soon as one gets the chance than to go head to head with a sociopath.

CHAPTER 9

Dealing with a Sociopath

Normal people possess a natural affinity for other individuals. This is why it is impossible to hurt someone without feeling at least the slightest pinch of guilt or remorse. Normal human beings naturally care for their fellow human beings. That's because we share the feelings of fear, anguish, suffering, and frustration.

There are times when we hurt the ones we love, although we do not mean to. In this case, the guilt is worse, because in addition to causing them pain, the remorse is heightened due to our affection for them. Our attachment with them makes the guilt over hurting them much worse. With a sociopath, such natural feelings of attachment and affection are non-existent, as are guilt, conscience, and empathy.

Sociopaths are More Common than you Think.

According to research, sociopaths comprise about four percent of the population. This goes to say that sociopaths are quite common. They are everywhere, and most of them are not so easy to detect. In fact, people who come into contact with sociopaths are in denial. They simply cannot admit that someone they thought they knew, someone they have trusted, is actually a sociopath incapable of love.

It is not easy to identify a sociopath. This is mainly because they are clever in building up their cover. But, there are a few questions that may lead you to clues that can help you detect a sociopath. The trouble here is that it may prove difficult to be objective in your assessment, especially when this person is someone close to you. In any case, you can ask yourself the following questions to help you compare this   person with others in your life and ultimately find out whether he or she is a sociopath or not.

- Does it feel like this person is only using you?
- Does it feel like this person does not really care about you?
- Does this person lie to you constantly?
- Does this person contradict his own statements or stories?
- Does this person take from you and never seem to have the intention of giving back?
- Does this person use pity?
- Does he make you feel sorry for him too often?
- Does this person make you feel guilty or turn the tables and make it appear like you are at fault?

- Does it feel like this person is taking advantage of your kindness?
- Does this person get easily bored?
- Does he seek constant stimulation?
- Does he often use flattery to get to your good side?
- Does this person make you feel worried?
- Does this person make you feel like he is entitled or like you owe him?
- Does this person tend to blame others for his mistakes?
- Does he refuse to acknowledge his own faults and take the blame?

Finally, does this person seem to do such things more than any other people in your life? If most of your answers are affirmative, then there is a good chance that you are indeed dealing with a sociopath. Even if he is not one, this person is clearly not good for you.

Dealing with a sociopath is not easy. Whether you are in a romantic or business relationship with this person, there are a few rules you must follow. Doing these things can help minimize the damage and the possible harm that may come your way.

Seek immediate help from a professional.

Unless you make an effort first to understand how a sociopath operates, you have a minimal chance of surviving a sociopath. A professional can help you learn the motivations and the tactics of a sociopath. A professional can help you understand that this person is different, not to mention the fact that they are very good at mind control.

Someone who specializes in sociopathy can help you understand how you have been trapped in a vicious cycle of deception and manipulation, and how it can be stopped. Finally, you can see through the illusion that the sociopath in your life has created. You will realize what the relationship is all about. In this way, you can stop this person from controlling you.

The moment you become aware of the sociopath's true identity is the same moment he starts to lose control and power over you. He may still try to, but the effects become minimal.

Stop making contact.

As long as you give the sociopath a chance, he will continue to make attempts to manipulate you. This makes it much wiser to stop contact completely. That means you should not call him, receive his calls, answer his emails, or even read his messages.

There is no hope of reasoning with a sociopath. Such a person is incapable of feeling the same emotions as normal people do. This person will feel no guilt for what he has put you through.

Do not try to give the sociopath any ultimatums. It will never work. You are bound to lose. The sociopath's advantage is his lack of guilt. So, do not waste any more energy trying to make peace with this person.

Once you make the attempt to flee from the sociopath, you must also inform the people around you about the situation. The tendency is for the sociopath to contact them and get on their good side. The sociopath is more likely to isolate you from the people you care about and to make it appear like you are the one with the big issue. You must stop it before it happens.

Do not share any more information.

After a while of being with the sociopath, he has more likely learned some information about you, your family, your work, and your friends. This information will be used and may have already been used against you. Remind yourself that you are dealing with a professional manipulator. Do not give him the chance to use any more information to take control of you.

Understand both your strengths and weaknesses.

Before leading you into his world, the sociopath has taken his time to learn about and understand your strengths and weaknesses. And, he has used this knowledge well. By understanding your strengths, and especially your weaknesses, you become more able to recognize the instances when the sociopath will make an attempt to press these buttons.

Stick to your instincts.

You may have seen the signs, but you may have given this person the benefit of the doubt. A sociopath is not worthy of such a benefit. You become subject to further manipulation and you are repeatedly dragged into the worst of situations when you continue to override your instincts.

Do not make any attempts at reformation.

It is important to understand that a sociopath does not think there is anything wrong with him. Treatment for sociopaths, especially for adults, is more often than not, useless. In fact, treatment may make them even worse than they already are.

Just like drugs can be misused, therapy can also be misused. Sociopaths abuse the privilege of therapy to get more information about people's behavior. You can trust that such information will be used for their advantage later.

You must accept the fact that a sociopath cannot change his very nature. In fact, sociopaths do not even recognize the need for change.

Realize none of it is your fault.

You have been tricked. That is the plain truth. This person has appealed to your good nature and has used you. If you continue to let him, he will drain you up. It is also important to realize and understand that none of this is your fault.

You should not blame yourself. So, be forgiving of yourself.

Of course, the story changes when the sociopath turns out to be someone who is part of your family. You are bound by blood and obligation. That means it is not an option to walk away. This does not mean, however, that you should let your guard down. Take the same precautions. Keep informed and seek help for you and your loved one.

CHAPTER 10

Is there Hope for a Sociopath?

Sociopaths share similar personality traits. But, there are different types of sociopaths too. Such includes the following.

The Entitled Sociopath

This type of sociopath is in a state of over self entitlement. For this sociopath, fulfilling his needs is of utmost important. He has no ideals. He is immune to shame. And, he is more likely to feel satisfaction in what he does. This sociopath likes to defy authority and actually feels proud of it.

The Amoral Sociopath

Lacking any sense of guilt, this sociopath bears no concept of morality. This sociopath often has a very weak capacity to feel pain. He has a primitive sense. He is incapable of acknowledging the pain that he inflicts to others. This sociopath is more likely to torture, and finds pleasure in watching others' pains.

The Common Sociopath

This sociopath makes up the majority of antisocial personalities. And, like other types of sociopaths, he feels no remorse for what would normally shame other people. He has either a weak or no sense of caring for the future. And, rather than observing the rules, this sociopath likes breaking them.

The Alienated Sociopath

This sociopath's ability to love is undeveloped. He feels no attachment to other people. He is unable to identify with others or care about them.

There are different types of alienated sociopath. One of them, the disempathic type, is capable of emotional investment. However, his circle of empathy is only limited to family members and other loved ones, including pets. People who are outside his circle of empathy are treated merely as objects.

The Aggressive Sociopath

This sociopath likes to feel empowered and has a strong sense of self importance. This is the kind of a sociopath who actually finds pleasure in hurting and threatening others. Dominance and control give them gratification.

In addition to becoming criminals, this sociopath's desire for interpersonal dominance may also be seen in police officers, bureaucrats, and even employers, educators, and parents. In this case, aggressive sociopathy can become one's personal style.

The Dyssocial Sociopath

This sociopath can be normal in both psychological and temperamental facets. He may be capable of feeling guilt and shame. This person may even be capable of loyalty. However, such feelings are only dedicated to the group he recognizes. And, it is a limited circle. Among the other types of sociopaths, this one has a higher chance of learning a different set of rules than what he grew up to adapt to.

So, is there hope for a sociopath?

First of all, it is important to bear in mind that the sociopath's brain is wired differently. This is something that is unfixable.

Sociopathy cannot be cured. However, at its early onset, the development into full-blown sociopathy may be prevented. Nevertheless, there are treatment options for sociopaths that can help them cope and recognize normal human emotions. Such treatments include social skills training, behavioral and cognitive therapy, medication, and physical treatments such as electroconvulsive therapy and neurosurgery.

These treatment options may help a sociopath cope and recognize social norms. It can enable them to live close to normal lives. The problem is, most sociopaths do not recognize the need for help, which can make treatments ineffective.

Not all sociopaths are intrinsically bad.

The second point that has to be made is that not all sociopaths are criminals. Not everyone is violent. There are actually high functioning sociopaths who contribute positively to society.

The idea of a "good" sociopath may be debatable. It may be close to saying that black magic can be good, too. Some sociopaths are capable of channeling their energy to become productive members of society, although this does not change the fact that they are far from normal.

Sociopaths should not be viewed in comparison to normal people. As mentioned previously, sociopaths have a different kind of wiring. Their brains have a different make-up. They cannot be blamed for being the way they are, for being and feeling different. However, the fact remains that they are completely responsible for making their choices, whether those choices result in good or bad.

CHAPTER 11

Narcissism Defined

The term "narcissism" was derived from the Greek myth about a hunter named Narcissus. He was the handsome and arrogant son of a god and a nymph. He was so attracted to his own reflection in the water that he did not leave it until he died.

Nowadays, narcissism is the term used to refer to all those who seek to satisfy the self as driven by one's own vanity. It is also defined as a strong approval and interest in the self, particularly in one's physical and intellectual characteristics. In a nutshell, narcissism is the result of haughtiness and pride.

Narcissists are especially fond of mirrors, as narcissists are concerned about how they look and wish to frequently monitor and admire their outward appearances. The narcissist also projects the aura of having a high level of self confidence, but lacks the humility of a balanced person.

One common tendency among narcissists is that they become very defensive when someone poses a threat to their self-esteem, and some narcissists even become increasingly hostile towards the source of such threats. Some narcissists use their bloated ego as an attempt to mask insecurity, while others actually feel highly satisfied with themselves and live an affectedly genteel lifestyle.

Narcissism is a subject of study in the social sciences due to its effects upon the self and society. There is, in fact, the acknowledgement of a healthy form of narcissism, and it should not be mistaken as being synonymous with egocentrism (which is more likened to being self-centered or selfish).

Oftentimes, the narcissist is physically attractive and charismatic when you first meet him or her. However, the longer you get to know a narcissist, the more you realize that they find it difficult to maintain healthy long-term relationships. Generally, narcissistic behavior dwindles once the person reaches the age of 30.

The Narcissistic Personality Disorder

Narcissism becomes a disorder once it disrupts the life of the individual and the people surrounding them. This is referred to as Narcissistic Personality Disorder, and it is more severe and less common than narcissism. Individuals who suffer from this condition feel that they are the center of the universe. Thus, they lack empathy, view themselves as the only priority, and constantly seek the attention and appreciation of others. The person who is perceived by many to be too self-assertive, selfish, manipulative, and needy is one who is highly likely to have this disorder.

Narcissists prioritize accomplishing extreme personal goals, such as becoming famous, and believe that they are entitled to being treated exclusively over everyone else. They tend to overestimate their capabilities and engage in risky and impulsive endeavors, as they believe that they can always come out the winner.

A narcissist does not hesitate to step on other people's toes to reach her goals, and often lies about her accomplishments, abilities, and importance. A narcissist often daydreams about becoming impossibly successful, powerful, attractive and intelligent. He is quick in temper, and becomes very jealous if the attention is diverted from him. At its extreme, the Narcissistic Personality Disorder leads a person to be incapable of feeling any emotions towards others.

Unfortunately, there is no absolute treatment for Narcissistic Personality Disorder, as narcissists deny their condition and do not seek clinical treatment. One way to help narcissists become more engaged and sincere towards others would be to include them in social groups and community activities.

The Possible Causes of Narcissism

It is an ongoing debate as to what causes narcissism. It may be due to both genetics and the environment. Narcissism may be the effect of inherent physical and intellectual traits. A physically appealing individual often feels superior to others, especially if this belief is reinforced by the people surrounding him or her. Narcissism may also be triggered by environmental influences, such as the admiration of a celebrity who also exhibits narcissistic traits.

According to Sigmund Freud, the development of narcissists can stem from how their parents treated them. Narcissists were often the ones who were either treated coldly or were given too much admiration by their parents; narcissism is even more likely to occur if a child is given a combination of both types of treatment. Future scholars of psychology lean towards this theory and further state that such inconsistency leads a person to feel insecure inwardly and react by bolstering their confidence as they seek the admiration of others. Peers also contribute to this inconsistency and further the development of narcissism, because they are initially attracted to the charisma of the narcissist but then shun him once they get to know him in the long run.

In truth, there are so many other factors that can come into play in regards to shaping the mind of a narcissist. You will learn more about these in the succeeding chapters.

Identifying a Narcissist

Contrary to popular belief, narcissism is not always easy to understand, because there are so many aspects to it. Actually, not all narcissists act as if they are the kings or queens of the world. Some of them are so manipulative that they can mask their haughtiness and fake interest in others, with the ulterior motive of getting everyone's attention.

Narcissism is sometimes channeled through excitement, aggression, or a mixture of both. If you take a look at the common traits among narcissists, you will find that they all have an overflow of self-confidence, self-absorption, self-praise, and grandiloquence.

The ongoing trends of modern culture, such as the ability to easily self-advertise online via social media networks, have strengthened the cultivation of narcissism. With such a phenomenon going on right now, it might even be more challenging to find a person who is not a narcissist than to find someone who is.

Conversing with a Narcissist

One way to find out if a person is a narcissist is simply to engage them in a conversation. If you start talking about a topic that does not focus on him, you will notice that the conversation will always go back to him talking about himself. The narcissist is also incapable of listening to someone else talk about topics that do not involve him.

As expected, the favorite topic of any narcissist is their own selves. If the conversation is about anything else, a narcissist will fight to gain the advantage by frequently interrupting the other speaker or letting them finish and then once again start talking about a completely different topic (which will most likely be about themselves again).

They are unable to empathize with anyone else and tend to brush off the stories and experiences of other people. Another thing that you will notice when you are in conversation with a narcissist is that they tend to namedrop a lot in order to make themselves sound superior. This can range from knowing the right people to having gone to prestigious schools and being part of exclusive clubs. Bragging is second nature to the narcissist.

The Narcissist's Relationships

You should also take a look at the relationships that a narcissist maintains. They often find it difficult to keep long-term and mutual relationships, and they usually have only trivial friendships. They tend to stick with people who constantly supply them with praises and admiration.

The Severity of Narcissism

When it comes to how they carry themselves, you will find that there are "mild" and "severe" narcissists. Some of them can actually be very approachable and charismatic in the superficial sense, but there are those who are snobs and have a fondness for putting down other people and talking about them behind their backs. The worst part is, narcissists are unaware of their condition, and so they tend to lack self-reflection. They feel that their behavior is normal and acceptable, and they find it hard to grasp when someone else does not find them likeable, attractive, and so on.

If you happen to be well-acquainted with a sociable narcissist, you will be quite mesmerized by how they carry themselves, and you might want to accompany them more frequently. Take care, though, as the narcissist often manipulates others in order to acquire their personal goals. More often than not, once a narcissist feels that you are of no use to them, they will simply dismiss you, and will not want anything to do with you.

The narcissist prefers to dwell in metropolises, with individualistic culture being the norm. They have a strong liking for entertainment that celebrates the self, such as reality TV shows, and their idea of leadership would be to dominate and exploit their subordinates instead of doing their part in the hard work.

Try to insult a narcissist, and you are in for a bitter war. They never like to listen to criticism, even the constructive kind. Some of them put on a face of seemingly accepting it with grace, but would then talk bitterly about the criticism and then attempt to justify their own behavior. A narcissist prefers to be admired over being liked by people, and when you tell them that they are not as intelligent or as attractive as they think they are, they will become very hostile.

Observe the body language of a person whom you think could be a narcissist. Usually, they carry themselves haughtily, constantly bearing an arrogant expression, especially when facing a possible threat to their self-esteem. They also tend to exaggerate their hand gestures during a conversation.

Furthermore, in order to determine whether a person is a narcissist or not, find out whether he expresses unconditional love to anyone else. Unconditional love is granted only upon those that one can gain nothing from, such as a helpless animal or senile relative. A narcissistic person will not bother to spend time with anyone or anything that will not help them satisfy their selfish desires.

The Secret Narcissist

A lot of people tend to think that narcissists are extroverted individuals. While this stereotype has a lot of truth to it, there are actually introverted narcissists as well. A lot in this book is dedicated to the extroverted narcissists, as they tend to be more influential, but in this chapter, you can take a peek at the mind of the secret narcissist.

According to psychologists, secret or "covert" narcissists pride themselves on being perceived as "sensitive" and "mysterious," when in reality, giving this impression is intended to mask their anxieties and vulnerability. In this sense, they are just as extremely needy as their extroverted counterparts.

The Traits of the Secret Narcissist

Secret narcissists easily become lost in thought regarding themselves and their many fears. They are very self-conscious when getting attention, but are eager to hog credit for an accomplishment, even if it was achieved with the help of other people. They feel that their concerns are too important for them to bother about the problems of others. They prefer to be alone, and only care to be in a group if the others openly accept and praise them. Just like the extroverted narcissist, secret narcissists easily get jealous of others, and would feel annoyed if someone started talking about another person to them.

The secret narcissist is often quick to judge, and rates others depending on how they treat him. Secret narcissists can also be aggressive and hostile, especially when they are criticized or have failed at something. Secret narcissists steer clear of any form of rejection. They also feel that they are always burdened, and they tend to have that "me against the world" thing going on.

One major reason why the secret narcissist is different from the more extroverted one is due to their ability to put up a façade in front of their real selves, thus making them somewhat more success-fully manipulative.

The Secret Narcissist vs Introversion

How does one distinguish between the secret narcissist and the naturally shy person? That is indeed a difficult task, as both individuals are mum about how they really feel inside. The secret narcissist pretends to be withdrawn, when in fact they are just very frustrated at how the rest of the world fails to recognize their brilliance. One way to tell the difference between the two is to find out what passions they have. For example, an introverted person who is genuinely interested in activities such as rescuing animals or volunteering for a charity is certainly not a secret narcissist. On the other hand, the seemingly quiet individual who has nothing to talk about except herself in her private blog may very well be a secret narcissist.

CHAPTER 12

The Narcissist in You

In light of the promotion of self-love, the distinction between having healthy self-esteem and having narcissistic tendencies should be spelled out clearly. After all, it is standard within society, particularly in urban communities, to have high self-esteem. It helps you pass job interviews, build networks, and accomplish piles of tasks on a daily basis, which makes it perfectly alright. It is a natural part of our personalities, a survival instinct. However, the moment a person starts to treat others manipulatively or in any other negative way for their personal pleasure, they are crossing over to the dark side of narcissism.

To put it bluntly, healthy self-esteem is all about being able to respect one's self. Narcissism, on the other hand, is all about seeking recognition due to the craving for attention and admiration. To the narcissist, these are drugs, and if the supply starts to run out, they will immediately find ways to get more.

A person with healthy self-esteem gets his or her strength from within, while the narcissist only feels good if he or she gets the approval of others. Having self-esteem is all about acknowledging your principles and respecting your role models, while narcissism leads its victims to set impossibly high standards for themselves and others around them. Narcissists tend to admire public figures who share similar character traits. Narcissism is all about the green-eyed monster; competition and comparison are the rules of the game. A narcissist prefers to be the dictator, while a person with healthy self-esteem leans on cooperation and equality.

Having self-esteem means believing in yourself without needing to brag to others about your abilities, while narcissism is all about braggadocio and putting down other people to make oneself seem more important in the eyes of others.

Development of Narcissism vs. Self-Esteem

Children whose parents praised them even if no effort was made are more likely to become narcissists. Such children grew up feeling pressured to be someone who should always find praise from others, making this their primary goal.

However, children who were raised by parents who responded genuinely to their actions would have a sense of awareness regarding themselves and their surroundings, thus developing healthy self-esteem.

According to studies, in order to avoid raising a narcissist, it is important to not dish out praises to children for talents that they do not have, or for skills that they have not honed. They should be complimented for real achievements in order to boost their self-esteem.

Of course, it is not just the parents who are to blame for the development of narcissism. Each society also has a critical role, particularly its culture. A society has certain cultural and social standards that either make a person feel better or worse about themselves. A person can also set the bar too high for themselves in terms of meeting those standards, end up getting disappointed, and cope in whatever ways they can, one of which is to become narcissistic.

For instance, in most parts in the West, an "ideal" man should be wealthy and successful, while the "ideal" woman is young and beautiful. These ideas can have severe effects on children, and coupled with other influences surrounding them, these ideals will affect how children view themselves and others.

Developing Self-Esteem Instead of Narcissism

The first thing you need to do is to recognize patterns in your behavior. Reflect upon the last time you have hurt someone, or how you reacted to criticism. Did you react defensively and start trying to justify your behavior? Narcissists tend to block out any thoughts and actions that make them feel insecure. But, in order to have healthy self-esteem, you need to take a look at it objectively, and own up to any mistakes in order to learn from the experience.

Learn to be more sensitive towards how other people feel. For example, be more patient with a person who cannot seem to understand a concept as quickly as you did, instead of gloating on your superiority.

A person is taught all his life to fight in order to survive, and striving to improve one's self has become the norm. While this is not entirely a bad thing, one should not beat himself up over failures and perceived imperfections. That way, healthy self-esteem is nurtured and narcissism is discouraged.

How do you find out if you are a narcissist? If you are, the chances are that you know of it. After all, every single person has a certain level of narcissism within them. Each person whether they admit it or not experience moments of narcissistic tendencies.

How do you find out if you are a narcissist? If you are, chances are that you already know of it. After all, every single person has a certain level of narcissism within them.   Each person, whether one admits it or not, experiences moments of narcissism.

Healthy Self-Love

It is not an entirely bad thing to like your own self. A lot of research has revealed that most people–about eighty percent–usually inwardly believe themselves to be better than the rest. This is healthy, in a way, for it helps us survive. This mindset allows us to acknowledge our personal strengths and depend on them in order to survive day by day.

A distorted perception of the self, on the other hand, is what the narcissist has. They overemphasize their strengths and believe themselves to have no weaknesses. Individuals with healthy minds occasionally find faults within themselves, which is another function of the human instinct to survive, for it helps that person to be open to change.

How Narcissistic Are You?

Now, the main concern is the severity of one's narcissism. To find out how narcissistic you are, ask yourself the following questions: Have you caught yourself constantly hyperbolizing your achievements or lying about them? Do you feel that you are better than most of the people around you, that you are more attractive, intelligent, or talented than they are? Do you treat the people around you in a haughty manner? Are your goals sky-high and almost–if not completely–impossible to reach? Are these goals all about attaining power, riches, success, and beauty?

You should also question yourself as to whether you have a strong desire for constant praise and attention, often catching yourself asking others if you are beautiful or if you are great at something. Also, if you feel that you have every right to be treated in a special way, look out. It is highly likely that you are a narcissist. Have you ever exploited someone in order to attain something that you wanted for yourself? How many times has this happened? Are you indifferent towards the feelings of other people?

If you happen to come across someone who is happy or grieving, do you catch yourself faking your emotions? If you said yes to most of these questions, then your level of narcissism is quite high. Think back on the times when you were envious of someone's accomplishments, as well as the times when you thought that someone was jealous of you, even if you have no proof. If you cannot seem to feel love towards another person, the kind of love wherein you still feel for them even though you will not get anything in return, then you may be highly narcissistic.

The Extreme Narcissist

Unfortunately, if you are the kind of person who is questioning his or her own narcissistic tendencies, then you are not an extreme narcissist. The reality is that extreme narcissists do not care about such self-reflections, for they consider themselves to be guiltless and would even find many of these questions insulting. After all, they do think that the universe revolves around them, so how could someone of less importance dictate their behavior? What they do know–and they can be quite proud of it–is that they are aggressive, power-hungry, and impulsive.

This certain level of self-awareness should not be mistaken for self-reflection, though, as the extreme narcissist does not like the idea of changing themselves. All they know is that the people who are "pulling them down" are either jealous or cannot fathom their splendor. The arrogance that a narcissist displays is their reaction to these so-called "haters."

What is even worse is that narcissism–being popular, beautiful, and mean–is perceived as a status symbol. Hollywood has emphasized the seeming correlation between meanness and being attractive. Thus, a person who is being called a narcissist who is arrogant and mean also believes him or herself to be attractive and the subject of envy. Think of the 2004 released movie "Mean Girls." The main character, Regina George, is a narcissist who is admired and feared by everyone.

If you take a look at the cult following of the film, there are many young adults who still look up to her despite her narcissistic traits. The fact is that narcissists prefer to be admired and feared rather than to be liked by everyone. They actually revel in being described as being assertive and ambitious and care little for being perceived as kind and caring.

An extreme narcissist tends to have a lot of new friends, but very few, if any, old ones. As previously mentioned, narcissists attract a lot of acquaintances, but the more they get to know who the narcissist really is, the less they want to be with that person. One interesting thing is that narcissists actually know about this, but they do not really care, for they will always believe that they deserve better company.

If you feel that you have strong narcissistic tendencies, do not despair, for there is still hope for you, which will be discussed in the next chapter.

Learning From Healthy Narcissism

While extreme narcissism will not help you establish strong and meaningful relationships, mild narcissistic traits can be beneficial for you in life. For instance, exhibiting self-confidence for as long as it is realistic can help people gain your trust.

Your self-confidence will give you the strength to face challenges and overcome them. You can channel your self-confidence in recreational activities such as performing on stage or delivering a speech. A healthy level of narcissism will not include the exploitation of others, but enables you to be consistent in your being friendly and outgoing.

Having healthy narcissism also enables you to respect yourself in such a way that you are being your own best friend. In other words, you are able to defend yourself against people who are indeed trying to put you down. There is also a sense of pleasure in appreciating one's self, the feeling of knowing that you are exactly the kind of person that you want to be.

CHAPTER 13

The Narcissists of Today

There are many factors that can contribute to narcissism. It is indeed possible that one's naturally good looks and smarts can attract a lot of attention, thus strengthening the self-love of a narcissist, which leads to the conclusion that it is often both the genes and environment that shape the mind of a narcissist.

Pop culture has been worshipping the concept of individualism so much that it has strengthened narcissism as well. The messages that come across in today's society are all in praise and support of the self: "you have every right to reach your potential", the YOLO trend (You Only Live Once), "me" time, and so on. Celebrities, athletes, and political figures also heavily influence the self-love culture due to the tremendous amount of attention that they are getting. Social media networks further encourage people to capture their self-love moments and show them to others, which makes everyone else think it is perfectly acceptable, so they follow suit.

The Epidemic of Narcissism

Truth be told, narcissism is indeed spreading fast. There have been so many changes in society, particularly in terms of technology, that have grown the narcissist's tendencies to magnificent proportions. This sharp increase is actually more notable in women, according to one study, although men still hold the trophy for the most number of blatant narcissists.

A recent survey that was conducted in order to check the prevalence of Narcissistic Personality Disorder has revealed that for every 10 young adults (individuals who are between 20 to 30 years of age), one has the disorder. It is notable that the number of cosmetic surgeries is skyrocketing, and even those who cannot afford it are willing to go in debt just to get it. Even the entertainment industry is displaying more and more personalities with extreme narcissistic traits, and audiences like it.

A US study conducted by personality researchers in 2012 shows that the current generation of young adults has the highest recorded number of narcissists of any generation so far; thus, the term "Me Generation" has been coined. According to research, most high school and university students of today are driven by selfish desires instead of selfless goals such as helping the environment and the community. This finding led the head researcher to conclude that narcissism is a widespread "disease" that is growing fast within society. However, this does not mean that everyone born from the 80's to the 2000's has the narcissistic bug in them.

It must be noted that each individual has his or her own unique personality, physical makeup, educational background, and social circles. The internet and social media can also affect how people view themselves and others around them.

The source of narcissistic behavior nowadays may also stem from contemporary culture's love of money. While money itself has also been the object of desire of many past generations, the current generation's desire to acquire money has grown so much because there is an even bigger need for it. There may also be a bigger need to be more concerned about one's image in society–from the looks to the curriculum vitae–because the struggle to compete against others for a job position has become even more challenging.

Another factor to look at in determining how one becomes a narcissist is how they were raised. Generally, Baby Boomers are more concerned with society in comparison to members of Generation X, if you trace back their respective behaviors and experiences. A Generation X parent may raise their children to be more self-loving compared to how the Baby Boomers raised them. Of course, that does not necessarily mean that Generation X does a bad job of being parents. It is possible that the trend among today's young adults of delaying marriage in order to pursue personal goals and explore abilities can help them to become better individuals that can influence the future generations.

Individuals have varying degrees of narcissistic traits within themselves, and people do change for the better or worse. Narcissism, as was mentioned in the previous chapters, reach particularly high levels before a person hits his or her 30s. In this day and age, when self-interest is increasingly becoming a socially acceptable norm, narcissistic tendencies are flourishing.

However, there is still hope, for as long as these tendencies fall into a pathological personality disorder, a person can actually outgrow his or her narcissistic ways. The saying "it's just a phase" can come into play here. There is a correlation between narcissism, age, and life experiences that change how a person views himself and society.

What you should never do to a narcissist is to humiliate them or be too blunt towards them, for it is more than their personality can take.

It is clear to many social scientists that the one who is hopeful to change the narcissist isn't the narcissist himself, but the person who genuinely cares for him. It must be made clear that in order for this change to occur, the narcissist must want it.

There are instances wherein a narcissist changes his ways if he has been subjected to a "humbling experience," but oftentimes, they will bounce back to their old ways as soon as they are able to recover. It is difficult for a narcissist to get out of the warped sense of reality, for it is their comfort zone, a place where they feel safe and secure. Any threat to this comfort zone will cause the narcissist to become very hostile, so tread carefully.

The Challenge of Changing the Narcissist

Many people who have been dealing with narcissists through most parts of their lives have accepted the fact that they rarely ever change. It is indeed difficult to convince a person to change who is already extremely satisfied with his or her personality. Narcissists are very happy with how they live their lives. If you want them to change, they will actually think that there is something wrong with you, and that you should be the one to change.

If you want to see a change in your narcissistic loved one, the first thing you need to do is to reflect upon yourself instead of thinking about the narcissist. You must accept the possibility that if you are unable to change him, you can instead make changes within your own life and outlook. If your narcissistic loved one is abusive, you should start saying no to the relationship. Otherwise, you too will become narcissistic.

To enable the narcissist to change, or at least to minimize their narcissistic tendencies, what you can do is to expose a narcissist to opportunities for empathy, which will enable them to become more sensitive towards people, and help them tone down their self-centeredness. One example would be for a narcissist to watch movies or documentaries that will show him the many other faces of humanity, helping him realize that he is a part of a bigger whole.

Give him the chance to talk to others who are less fortunate than himself, and allow him to extend a helping hand. If there is little to no response regarding this, then you would have to turn the tables by using the narcissist's own weaknesses against him to make him change. He will only seek to change himself if he sees that this change will personally benefit him and offer him what he desires so much– power, control, and attention.

Although society is very much fascinated with the tools that breed narcissism within it–from social media networks, with the constant flow of communication and photo posts, to reality TV–action must be taken into consideration in order for this so-called narcissism epidemic to subside. While a healthy level of self-love is encouraged, failure to empathize and do one's part as an active member of the community is not advocated.

CHAPTER 14

How to Deal with a Narcissist

Narcissism does not sound lovely at all, so naturally, you would feel the need to avoid narcissists. However, there will be multiple times in your life when you will have to face them or even spend a part of your life with them. It could be your mother-in-law, your boss, or even your new roommate. It won't entirely be a bad thing to spend some time with a narcissist, as long you know how to deal with them.

For instance, the narcissist as a leader is very much a control freak. He is very charismatic and manipulative, showcasing his abilities to society with false bravado. The narcissistic leader is capable of extended networking and is prone to do so because he wants the attention and admiration of as many people as possible. Narcissistic leaders tend to lose their temper when they feel that control and power are slipping from their fingers, or if they are no longer included in social activities.

Keep in mind that many successful organizations and businesses have narcissistic leaders. It isn't a wonder, for they have the charm and confidence to pull it off. Expect them to blow their top off, sometimes unconscionably. Every now and then you will find that you and all the other subordinates are doing the more gruelling parts of the work.

In order to deal with the narcissist in your life, one thing that you can do is to butter them up. This is a great tactic if you want to manipulate the narcissist, who is a manipulator himself. If you think that you can't pull it off, remind yourself of the real reason behind it.

Be realistic when setting expectations with a narcissist. Keep in mind that they are artful manipulators, so they are definitely going to try and weasel their way into turning things in their own favor. If you have to work or live with a narcissist, you have to set boundaries very clearly with him up front.

Allow the narcissist to soak up all of the attention, especially when you want him to help out. Narcissists are notorious for being poor performers, but when placed in the limelight, they will do whatever it takes to gain favor. Keep in mind that they do not like to work in a group, so if they have to pitch in, you can tell them that you're posting stuff online about the team effort, and let the magic unfold.

On the other hand, avoid threatening their egos, because they may turn to aggression. There have been several cases of narcissists exacting revenge upon those who have openly criticized them. Choose your words very wisely in providing feedback to a narcissist. One piece of advice would be to make your tone sound light and humorous when providing feedback to a narcissist. Since narcissists use humor as a tool to get attention and admiration, you can use it on them as well to get your point across.

CONCLUSION

Thanks again for purchasing this book!

Psychopaths are a very fascinating subject for "normal" people, mostly because they are capable of committing unimaginable and often horrifying acts.

However, it is easy to confuse psychopaths with regular criminals because media and other social institutions have blurred the lines between the facts and myths about psychopathy. I hope that that book has been able to help you better understand the concept of psychopathy.

Not all psychopaths should be feared. In fact, many of them should be pitied—especially those psychopaths who mingle with normal people without really connecting with them.

While they are incapable of feeling negative emotions, they are also incapable of feeling love and attachment. When you think about that, psychopathy is the loneliest type of existence for any human being —only psychopaths themselves don't realize that.

Remember, the information contained in this book is strictly for educational purposes. It is in no way intended to instruct people on how to clinically identify psychopaths, nor should it be used to imitate the horrendous acts perpetrated by some of the world's worst psychopaths.

I hope the information presented here has given you a new, clear perspective about sociopathy. As researchers note, four percent of the general population are sociopaths. In other words, the chance of encountering one is not impossible.

In dealing with a sociopath, understanding his or her nature is the first step. And, may the things shared in this book become helpful to you along the way. Armed with the right information, you can better protect yourself if it becomes necessary.

Second, sociopathy is a heavy cross to bear. It stays with a person for the rest of his lifetime. While full-blown sociopathy may be quite impossible to correct, stopping the development of sociopathy is perfectly possible at its early onset. Awareness of the warning signs can help you prevent a loved one from turning out differently than the rest.

Finally, please bear in mind that not all sociopaths are created the same. Their lack of guilt, shame, and remorse, as well as their self centeredness and lack of empathy for others may be their common denominators. But, not all of them have criminal tendencies.

Sociopaths may be different. But some of them manage to do better than what is expected of them.

Narcissism is indeed a very interesting topic, not just for social scientists, but for the rest of the world as well. It is widely present, and it is also spreading out fast. You also may have noticed that, as society continues to change, the views and behaviors of narcissists also adapt to it. Their consistency is in their exceptional admiration of themselves, as well as their constant need for the approval of others.

Remember to cultivate healthy self-esteem within yourself and your community in order to become more sensitive towards each other. Narcissism may seem so captivating at first, but it will definitely not benefit the narcissist. Developing good habits, such as self-reflection and being open-minded, is key to avoid becoming narcissistic. In this world full of online status updates, pictures of digitally modified ideals, and the increased acceptance of public boasting, maintaining a healthy self-confidence has become all the more challenging. Remember that self-esteem is all about believing in yourself, the quiet kind of assurance that does not require anyone's approval.

Hopefully, this book has succeeded in its goal of broadening your understanding of personality disorders and mental illnesses, and may it also aid you in coping with the the tendencies that surround yourself and your loved ones.

One thing to remember about mental illness is that diagnoses of most conditions are based on what is normal or accepted in a culture. While severe anxiety is considered a mental condition in some countries, it is disregarded in others. In undeveloped places, mental disorders are perceived as possessions, curses, or results of witchcraft. However, only professionals can diagnose mental illnesses.

Mental illness is a sickness of the mind, an imbalance in the functioning of a person's brain that causes them to behave differently than others. As explained in the book, personality disorders are a kind of mental illness. The difference is that the character-istics are not morbid or altered versions of the normal personalities of humans, which is the case with most mental illnesses. Personality disorders are just as irrational as most mental illnesses, but the character-istics are within "sane" jurisdiction. They are, however, extreme versions of the average human personalities.

People with mental disorders do not suffer from them by choice. Much like other medical conditions, mental illnesses are caught or passed on, but most of all, they are developed. Afflicted people should not be judged or scorned. It is much harder for them to cope for reasons not everyone can understand. Their ability to comprehend is limited, and their thinking is clouded, disorganized, and disbelieving. It takes months to years of mental repair for them to be able to live like normal individuals.

They should be treated with sympathy as opposed to neglect, disrespect, or discrimination. Knowledge of mental illness will give us an understanding of what plagues the mentally ill and how the illness befell them. It will provide relatives and loved ones with what they need in order to support the afflicted person. It may not generate sympathy, but it will certainly discourage negative outlooks and treat-ments of the mentally ill.

With the help of this e-book, one can also determine signs, symptoms, and causes of mental illnesses. This will help one to determine whether internal issues are possible impending personality disorders or simply seasonal problems. It may enlighten those who have been suffering from a mental disorder without knowing of it and encourage them to seek help from loved ones or professionals.

In conclusion, one should not take recurring depressive states or dissocial characteristics lightly or discriminate upon those who experience them. One cannot know if this might be a sign of mental illness or a trigger for it.

Thank you,

Clarence T. Rivers

PS. If you enjoyed this book, please help me out by kindly leaving a review!